The Complete Photo Guide to

SLIPCOVERS,
PILLOWS & BEDDING

**Creative Publishing
international**

First published in the United States of America by
Creative Publishing international, Inc., a member of
Quayside Publishing Group
400 First Avenue North
Suite 400
Minneapolis, MN 55401

1-800-328-3895
www.creativepub.com

Visit www.Craftside.Typepad.com for a behind-the-scenes peek at our crafty world!

ISBN: 978-1-58923-690-5

10 9 8 7 6 5 4 3 2 1

Digital edition published in 2014
eISBN: 978-1-61058-420-3

Library of Congress Cataloging-in-Publication Data
available

Copy Editor: Kari Cornell
Proofreader: Karen Levy
Photography: Teresa Bennett, pg. 28 to 35; Therese M. Davis, pg. 68 to 83; rau + barber , pg. 100–107, 110, 112–122, 124–141, 144–163, 168–177
Cover Image: Courtesy of Bujor Handmades/
    www.bujorprov.com

Printed in China

The Complete Photo Guide to

SLIPCOVERS,
PILLOWS & BEDDING

Creative Publishing
international

CONTENTS

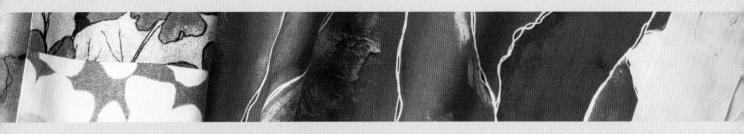

Introduction

Sewing for your home is one of the most meaningful and expressive ways to impart your personality and style in every room. Doing it yourself gives you the freedom to choose colors, fabrics, and design features in combinations that are not offered or may be difficult to find in stores or online. If you've ever shopped for bedding to coordinate with the existing wall colors and window treatments in a bedroom, you understand ready-made limitations. And when it comes to slipcovers, ready-made options are fashioned to fit only a few basic styles, so you may be stuck with ill-fitting covers made in fabric choices that are severely limited.

DIY home sewing is obviously less expensive than paying for custom-made soft furnishings, but it can also be thriftier than buying ready-made. The money you save in labor costs can be spent on higher-quality fabric or a few extra decorator pillows.

REVIVING YOUR FURNITURE WITH SLIPCOVERS

You don't have to buy new furniture to give your home a new look. In fact, you may love your furniture's style and the way it fits you, but you've grown a little tired of the color or pattern. Slipcovers give your furniture a fresh start when you want to change the color scheme of a room, update faded or worn upholstery, or simply alter the ambiance with the changing of the seasons.

Slipcovers can also modify the style of your furnishings a bit. You are limited somewhat by your furniture's original line—a wing chair will always be a wing chair—but you can make a slipcover that changes the look considerably. Unmatched pieces of furniture you've acquired at sales or secondhand shops can be slipcovered in matching or coordinating fabrics to unify them.

If that favorite chair still has firm padding and a sturdy frame, a custom-fitted slipcover is a great alternative to reupholstering it. Hugging the chair like a glove, a fitted slipcover gives the chair new life without changing its identity and without the added work of stripping the original cover and reupholstering. With slipcovers, family heirlooms and cherished antiques can retain their valuable "first skin" while playing an active role in the decorating plan.

The projects in this book use typical furniture candidates for slipcovers with variations in fabrics, skirt styles, and closures. You can mix and match techniques to design slipcovers that are just right for your furniture and décor. Various methods of slipcovering will be explored, each with step-by-step instructions. Experienced slipcover makers often work directly with the decorator fabric, which saves them time. But by making a muslin pattern, you're able to keep the pattern to make additional slipcovers from the same type of fabric at another time. Some slipcovers are easy to make, requiring only measuring the furniture and cutting the fabric into rectangles. Separate cutting instructions are provided for many of the projects. For some slipcovers, the cutting directions are incorporated into the instructions. Always read the You Will Need to Know section for important information specific to the project.

SEWING PILLOWS, BEAN BAG CHAIRS, TUFFETS, AND BEDDING

Pillows are among the easiest sewing projects and they require only a small amount of fabric, yet they provide comfort and decorative punch for bedrooms, dens, and living rooms. Using the techniques shown in this book, you can design countless pillows in a wide range of fabrics, with edge treatments and embellishments to suit any décor and budget.

Snuggle up with a book in a beanbag chair or put up your feet on a tuffet. These comfortable and stylish soft furnishings are easy and inexpensive to make. They are also great for rec rooms, children's bedrooms, and dorm rooms.

Sew bedding ensembles to dress up your bedrooms. Choose from a variety of styles, including duvet covers with coordinating pillow shams and bed skirts, lined and unlined coverlets, and full bedspreads. When you sew them yourself, you can choose fabrics in textures, colors, and patterns you like. Make duvet covers in washable, lightweight fabrics for comfort and ease of care. Design bedspreads in silk fabric with rayon cording for a formal master bedroom.

HOW TO USE THIS BOOK

Each project includes a materials list of everything you'll need. The list doesn't specify how much fabric to purchase because that will depend on the size of your furniture or mattress and the size of the pattern repeat for the printed fabric. The list doesn't include general sewing supplies like T-pins, glass head pins, fabric shears, straight edge for measuring, fabric markers, sewing machine, foot attachments such as zipper or cording foot, thread, iron, and pressing surface. Each project does include cutting directions and some advice to help you choose fabric and embellishments. Step-by-step instructions are accompanied by photographs to help you make slipcovers, pillows, and bedding you'll be proud to show in your home.

If you come across any unfamiliar words or phrases, check out the Terms to Know list on page 188.

SLIPCOVERS

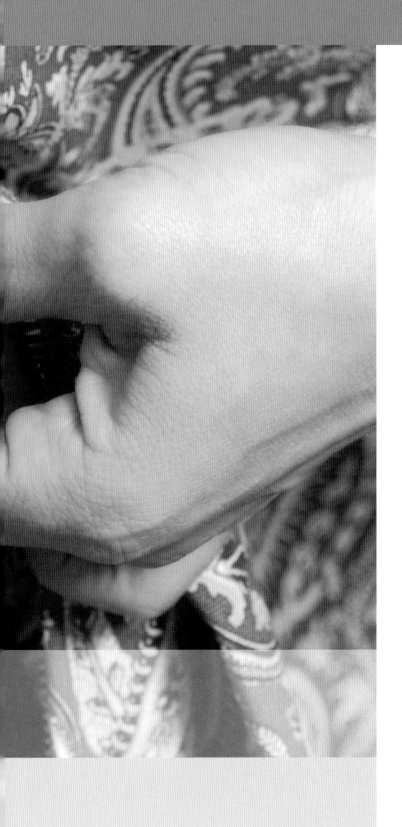

The techniques and projects in this section begin with the easiest slipcovers and progress to higher difficulty levels. While you are not likely to work your way through in order, it is helpful to read through all of the instructions and study the photographs. Skills learned in the easier projects are likely to help you understand and execute the techniques for more complicated projects.

Reversible Seat Cover

Give your dining room or kitchen chairs a fresh look with simple seat covers. Made with two coordinating decorator fabrics, these covers can be flipped over for an instant décor change. Darts sewn at the front corners shape the covers to fit the chair seats smoothly. The back corners are held in place with a button tab that wraps around the back of the leg.

WHAT YOU NEED TO KNOW

These covers wrap over all four edges of the seat, so they are suitable for armless chairs with straight sides and fronts that are open between the back posts. Because the amount of fabric needed depends on your chair size and the fabric design size, make the pattern first so you'll know how much fabric to purchase.

When making covers for two or more chairs, center the same motif on each seat cover. If you choose fabric with large motifs, such as the toile used on page 10, take the pattern with you when you shop for fabric.

YOU WILL NEED

- polyester muslin for making patterns

- two coordinating decorator fabrics, such as print and a stripe; amount depends on chair size and fabric design size

- four buttons for each cover, 7/8" to 1" (2.3 to 2.5 cm) in diameter (snaps or hook-and-loop tape can be used instead of buttons)

- ½ yd (0.5 m) grosgrain ribbon, 7/8" (2.3 cm) wide, in a color to match the fabrics

Reversible Seat Cover Pattern

1. Measure the chair seat side-to-side and front-to-back. Add 10" (25.5 cm) in each direction. Cut muslin to this size to make a pattern. Press the muslin pattern in half in both directions. Unfold. Center the pattern on the chair seat, allowing it to fall down over the front and sides. At the back, turn the pattern up along the posts. If necessary, tape the pattern in place with a nonsticky tape.

2. Mark a dot at one front cover. Pinch the fabric together from the dot down, bringing the front to meet the side. Pin out excess fabric, inserting the pins parallel to the chair leg to form a dart. Mark lines on both sides of the dart from the dot down to the bottom. Repeat on the other front cover.

3. Mark dots at the back of the seat and at the inside front corners of the back posts. (If your posts are round, mark each dot at a point in line with the front and side of the post.) Trace the outline of the chair seat on the pattern.

4. Remove the pattern from the chair; remove the pins. Draw lines 4½" (11.3 cm) outside the traced seat lines. At the back corners, draw lines from the dots to the outer lines to form squares. (These will be the stitching lines.) Mark pivot points (shown in blue) on the stitching lines ½" (1.3 cm) from the outer edge. Draw cutting lines (shown in red) ½" (1.3 cm) outside the stitching lines at the legs and the front darts. Fold the pattern in half to make sure it is symmetrical, and make any necessary corrections. Cut out the pattern on the outer lines.

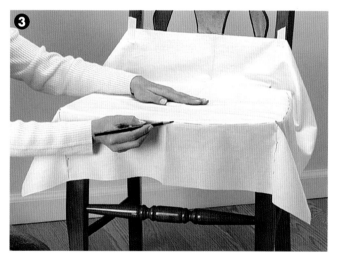

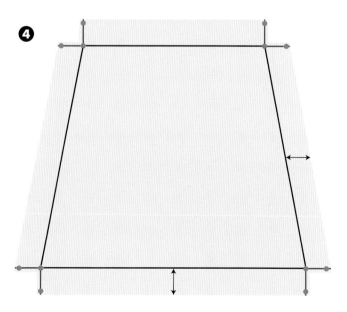

5. Place the muslin pattern on the top fabric, aligning the front-to-back crease with the crosswise grain. If using a large print, position the pattern so that the intersection of the creases is at the exact center of the design motif. Cut out seat cover top. Transfer the pivot points and dart dots to the wrong side of the fabric.

6. Cut out the remaining seat cover tops, using the front piece as a guide. This will make it easier to center the design motifs. Place each of the tops on the bottom fabric, right sides together. Pin near the outer edges. Cut them out; remove the pins.

7. Fold the dart on one front corner, right sides together, aligning the raw edges; pin. Stitch the dart.

(continued)

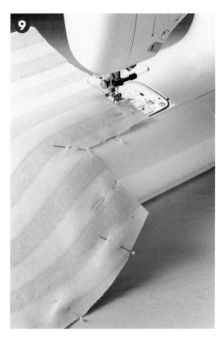

8. Repeat step 7 for the remaining front corners on the top and bottom pieces. Press the seam allowances of the darts open.

9. Place the top and bottom seat covers right sides together, aligning the raw edges; pin. Align the seams of the front darts. Stitch the layers together ½" (1.3 cm) from the edge all around, pivoting at the corners. Leave a 6" (15 cm) opening along one straight edge for turning.

10. Trim the seam allowances diagonally at the outer corners. Clip to, but not through, the stitches at the inner corners.

11. Turn back the top seam allowances and press, applying light pressure with the tip of the iron down the crease of the seam. In the area of the opening, turn back and press the seam allowances ½" (1.3 cm) where they meet.

12. Turn the cover right-side out through the opening. Insert a point turner or similar tool into the opening and gently push the pivot points out to form perfect corners. Push the seam out so that it is centered all around the outer edge and then press. Align the folded edges of the opening and pin them closed.

13. Edgestitch around the seat cover, stitching the opening closed; pivot at the corners.

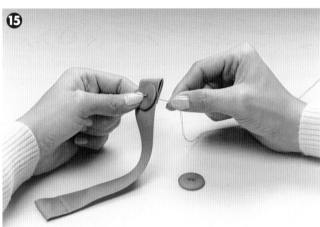

Helpful Hints

Press seam allowances open before turning a lined piece right-side out to make the seams lay smoothly along the edge. Often this means pressing the upper layer back, as in step 11.

Instead of buttons, attach Velcro or snaps to the ribbon tabs. Instead of ribbon tabs, insert grommets into the back corners and tie them around the chair legs with ribbon or decorative cord.

14. Mark placement lines for the four buttonholes parallel to and 1" (2.5 cm) above the lower side and back edges. Mark lines that equal the diameter plus the thickness of the buttons, with one end 1" (2.5 cm) from the vertical edges. Attach a buttonhole presser foot or buttonhole attachment. Stitch the buttonholes over the marked lines. Cut the buttonholes open, using a buttonhole cutter or small, sharp scissors.

15. Place the cover on the chair seat. At the back of one chair leg, measure the distance between buttonholes. Cut ribbon 4" (10 cm) longer than this measurement. Turn under 1" (2.5 cm) twice on each end of the ribbon; press. Stitch across the inner folds, forming double-fold hems. Stitch a button to the center of each hem. Repeat for the other leg. Button the chair seat cover in place.

Kitchen and Dining Chairs

Two-piece slipcovers for armless kitchen or dining room chairs update your décor and soften the room with fabric. Slipcovers are also a great way to renew worn or unmatched chairs. This slipcover style can range from shabby chic to tailored and formal, depending on the fabric choice and detailing of the cover.

WHAT YOU NEED TO KNOW

Both pieces of this slipcover are lined for durability and body. Welting, applied around the seat slipcover and along the lower edge of the back slipcover, defines and supports the edges.

These covers wrap over all four edges of the seat, so they are suitable for armless chairs that are open between the back posts and have straight sides and fronts. Decorative ties are secured to the back posts; concealed twill-tape ties secure the cover to the front legs of the chair.

The back slipcover and the skirt on the chair seat can be any length you want. For back slipcovers that are long, the back of the chair must be straight to the upper edge or tapered only slightly inward; if the top of the chair back is wider than the bottom, it will not be possible to slip the cover on. To help you decide on the best length for your project, take into account the style and detailing of the chair. For a nice drape and an attractive appearance, make the skirt at least 5" to 6" (12.8 to 15 cm) long and end the skirt slightly above or below any cross pieces of the chair. The seat slipcover can be made with either clustered gathers, as shown opposite, or pleats at the front corners, like the Parsons chair (page 25) and the ottoman (page 49).

Cutting Directions

1. Make the seat and back patterns according to the directions, below and opposite. Cut one seat each from the decorator fabric and the lining; transfer the marks. Cut one front and one back from both the decorator fabric and the lining; transfer the marks.

2. For a gathered skirt, cut the fabric as on page 20, steps 1 and 2.

3. Cut 1⅝" (4 cm) bias strips for welting. The combined length of the strips is equal to the circumference of the seat cover and the lower edge of the back cover; allow extra for seams and overlaps.

4. Cut eight fabric strips 1½" (3.8 cm) wide and 10" to 16" (25.5 to 40.5 cm) long for the back ties on the seat cover. Cut four 12" (30.5 cm) lengths of twill tape for the concealed front ties.

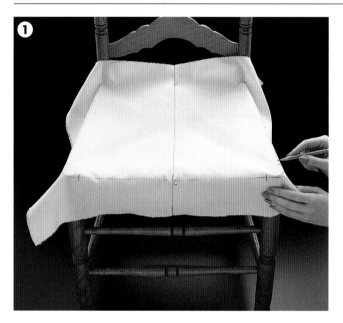

Chair Seat Slipcover Pattern

1. Measure the chair seat side-to-side and front-to-back. Add 6" (15 cm) in each direction. Cut muslin to size. Mark the center line on the lengthwise grain. Center the muslin on the seat; pin or tape in place. Using a pencil, mark the outer rim of the seat front and sides to back posts, rounding square corners slightly. Mark the placement for front ties.

2. Mark the back edge of the chair seat on the muslin; clip the fabric as necessary for a snug fit if the seat is shaped around back posts. Mark the placement of the skirt back between the chair posts.

3. Remove the pattern from the chair. Redraw seam lines as necessary, using a straightedge; redraw curved lines, drawing smooth curves. Reposition the pattern on the chair to check the fit; adjust as necessary.

4. Add ½" (1.3 cm) seam allowances to the pattern and cut it out.

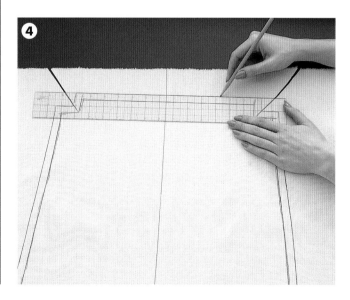

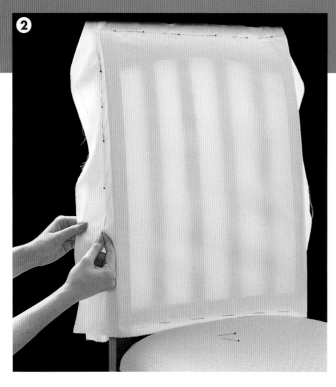

Chair Back Slipcover Pattern—
Straight Upper Edge

1. Measure the chair back; cut two pieces of muslin about 6" (15 cm) wider and 2" (5 cm) longer than the measurements. Mark a line 1" (2.5 cm) from the edge for the chair back; pin the pieces together on the marked line. Center the muslin on the chair with the marked line at the upper edge.

2. Pin the muslin at the sides of the chair, allowing ample ease. Mark the desired finished length. Pull gently on the cover to make sure it slides off easily; adjust the width or length of the cover, if necessary.

3. Mark the seam lines, following pin placement. Label the patterns for front and back.

4. Remove the muslin from the chair. Redraw the seam lines if necessary, using a straightedge. Repin the muslin, and position on the chairs; adjust as necessary. The front and back of the pattern may be different sizes.

5. Mark ½" (1.3 cm) seam allowances; mark the grain line. Cut out the pattern.

Shaped Upper Edge

1. Measure the chair back; cut two pieces of muslin about 6" (15 cm) larger than these measurements. Pin pieces together at the upper edge, and center over the chair back; adjust pins to follow contours of the chair, simplifying design as necessary. Continue as for chair back with straight upper edge, steps 2 to 4; in step 4, smooth any curved lines. Complete the pattern as in step 5.

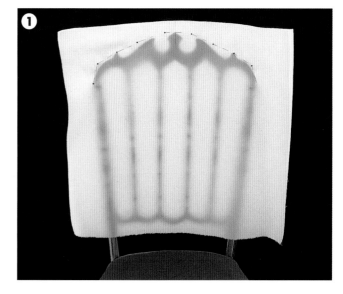

Sewing the Chair Seat Slipcover

1. Measure the pattern seam line around the front and sides of the seat between markings at the back posts; add 12" (2.5 cm) for seam allowances. Cut the fabric strip for the front skirt to this length, piecing fabric, if necessary; the width of the strip is equal to twice the desired finished skirt length plus 1" (2.5 cm) for seam allowances.

2. Measure the pattern seam line between markings for the back skirt. Cut the fabric strip for the back skirt to this length plus 1" (2.5 cm); the width of the strip is equal to twice the desired finished skirt length plus 1" (2.5 cm) for seam allowances.

3. Staystitch any inner corners and curves on the chair seat top and lining. Clip to, but not through, the stitching as necessary.

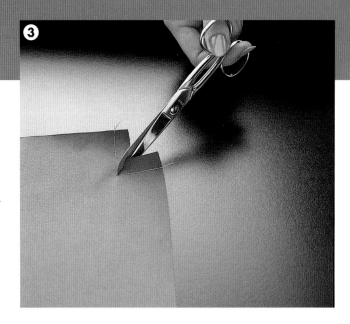

4. Make welting, if desired, and apply to the seat top as on page 184. Place two tie strips right sides together, stitch ¼" (6 mm) seam on the long sides and one short end of the tie. Trim corners and turn right-side out; press. Pin the ties to the right side of the seat top at the back corners, aligning the raw edges.

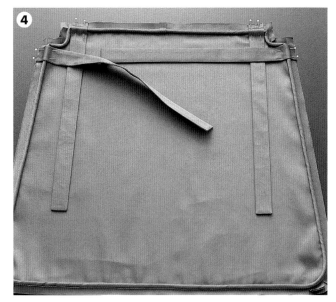

5. Fold the skirt front in half lengthwise, right sides together; stitch ½" (1.3 cm) seams on the short ends. Turn right-side out; press. Repeat for the skirt back.

6. Pin-mark the center of the skirt at the raw edges. Measure the edge of the seat pattern on the seam line, from center front to corner; add 3" (7.5 cm). Measure this distance out from the center of the skirt, and pin-mark for corners. Clip-mark the skirt 6" (15 cm) from both sides of the corner pin marks.

7. Stitch two rows of gathering threads along the upper edge of the skirt front between the clip marks, ¼" (6 mm) and ½" (1.3 cm) from the raw edges.

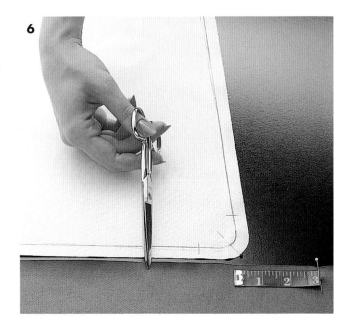

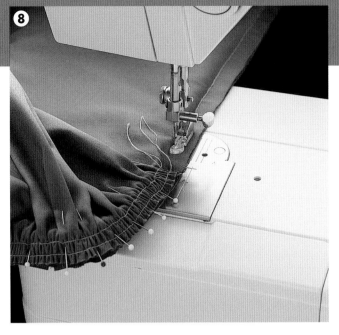

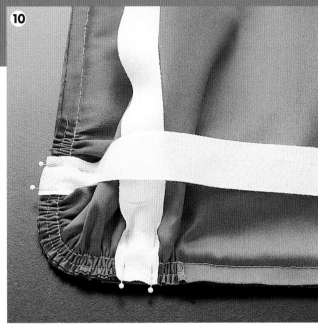

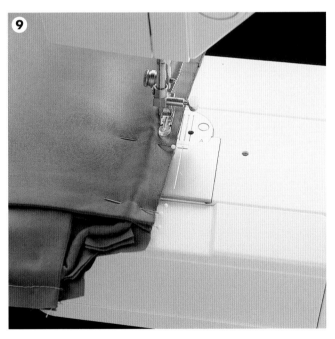

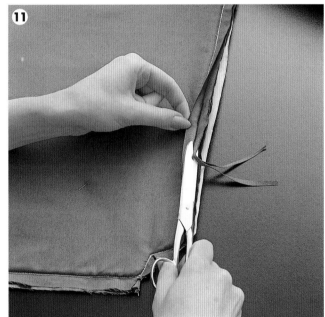

8. Pin the skirt front to the seat top, right sides together, matching the raw edges and markings for center front and corners. Pull the gathering threads to fit. Machine-baste the skirt to the seat top, using the upper zipper foot.

9. Pin the skirt back to the seat top, right sides together, matching the raw edges; stitch.

10. Pin or baste twill-tape ties to the wrong side of the skirt at front-corner marks.

11. Pin the skirt and ties to the seat to prevent catching them in the seams. Pin the lining to the seat, with right sides together and raw edges even. Stitch, leaving a 6" (15 cm) center opening in the back. Trim seam allowance; clip the curves and corners.

12. Turn the seat cover right-side out; press. Slipstitch the opening closed. Position the seat cover on the chair; secure the back ties in a bow or square knot. Lift the skirt, and secure the front ties; trim any excess tie length.

Sewing the Chair Back Slipcover—Straight Upper Edge

1. Place the front and the back decorator fabric pieces right sides together, matching the raw edges. Stitch ½" (1.3 cm) seam around the sides and upper edge. Press the seam open.

2. To accommodate the thickness of the chair back, open the corners, aligning the seam allowances; stitch across the corners a distance equal to the thickness of the chair back. Trim the seam.

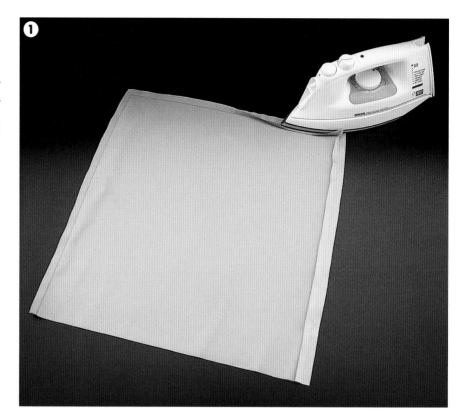

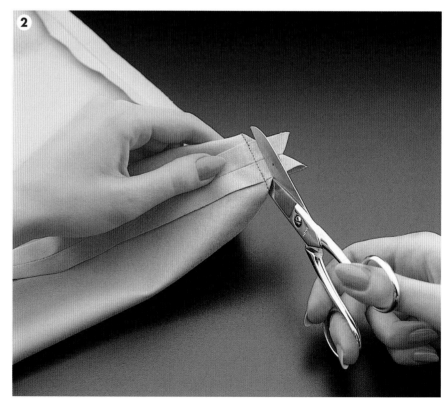

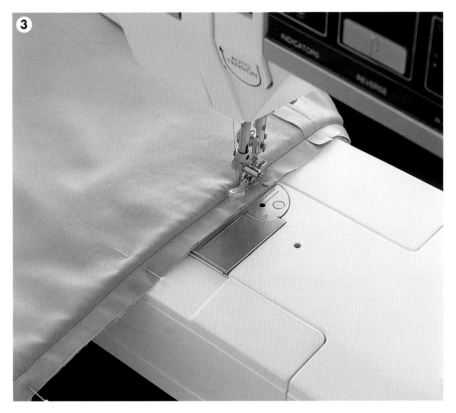

3. Attach the welting, if desired, to the lower edge of the outer cover as on page 184, steps 2 through 5. Stitch the lining as for the outer cover, leaving a 6" (15 cm) center opening on one side. Press the seam allowances open.

4. Place the decorator fabric and lining right sides together, matching the lower edge; stitch ½" (1.3 cm) seam.

5. Turn the slipcover, lining-side out, through the opening in the lining; press the lower edge. Slipstitch the opening closed. Turn the slipcover right-side out; place over the back of the chair.

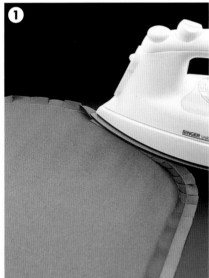

Shaped Upper Edge

1. Place the front and back decorator fabric pieces right sides together, matching the raw edges. Stitch ½" (1.3 cm) seam around the sides and upper edge; press open. Trim the seam; clip any curves. Complete as in steps 3 through 5 for straight upper edge.

Parsons Chairs

Parsons chairs are popular dining room chairs, with upholstered backs that adjoin upholstered seats. The lines are very tailored and straight. They have exposed wooden legs or upholstered legs. These one-piece slipcovers have skirts with inverted box pleats at the corners, and you may choose to make a slipcover with a short or floor-length skirt.

WHAT YOU NEED TO KNOW

These covers are suitable for chairs with straight backs. The upper edge of the chair back must be no wider than the lower back, or it won't be easy to slip the cover on. When measuring the front and back of the chair back, measure as if there were centered side seams, even if the seams on the upholstered chair are not centered.

The skirt for this style is self-lined, eliminating any noticeable hemline and giving the skirt extra body.

There are commercial patterns available for making Parsons chair slipcovers. If using a commercial pattern, be sure to measure carefully and make adjustments to the pattern before cutting your fabric, as Parsons chairs vary in size.

Pin-fitting the Pattern

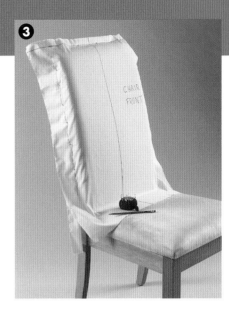

1. Measure the length and width of the front of the chair back. Add 4" (10 cm) to the length and the width. Cut muslin to size. Mark a center line on the lengthwise grain. Mark a line 1" (2.5 cm) from the raw edge at the upper edge on the muslin.

2. Repeat step 1 for the back of the chair back. Label the pattern pieces.

3. Pin the front and back pattern pieces of the chair back, wrong sides together, at the upper marked line, matching the center lines. Center the patterns on the chair back and pin the patterns at the sides of the chair, allowing ample ease. Mark the side seams on both the front and the back pieces.

4. Measure the length of the chair seat from the back to where the cushion meets the frame at the front. Measure the width from where the cushion meets the frame at the sides. Cut muslin 6" (15 cm) larger than measurement. Mark a center line on the lengthwise grain. Label the pattern piece.

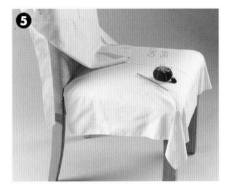

5. Press under 1" (2.5 cm) along the back of the chair seat pattern perpendicular to the center line. This will become the stitching line. Center the pattern on the chair seat with the pressed fold even with the chair back and smooth the fabric in place. Pin out excess fabric at the front corners, forming darts. Mark the dart seam lines with a pencil.

6. Mark dots on the front of the chair back pattern and on the fold of the chair seat pattern where the patterns meet at the outer edges of the seat back. Cut straight up from the bottom to the dots on the front chair back piece, allowing the fabric to spread so the side can be smoothed downward and the center bottom between dots can be smoothed forward under the seat pattern.

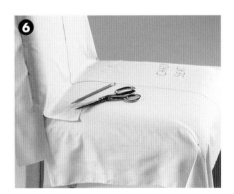

7. Pin the seat pattern to the front chair back pattern at the sides. Mark the seam on the front chair back piece between dots, even with the fold of the seat pattern. Continue marking the seam line down the sides of the front chair back even with the fold of the seat pattern.

8. Measure the distance from the floor to where the seat cushion meets the frame at the chair front. Record the measurement. Mark a seam line on the patterns all around the chair at this height from the floor.

9. Remove the patterns from the chair and redraw seam lines as necessary. Reposition the patterns on the chair; adjust as necessary. Add ½" (1.3 cm) seam allowances to all pattern pieces. Cut out the patterns.

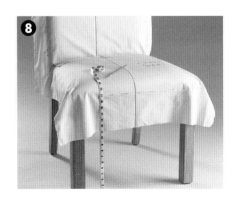

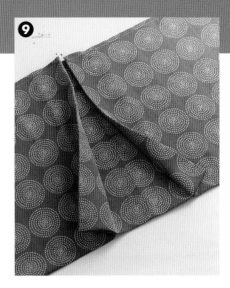

Sewing the Slipcover

1. Using the muslin patterns, cut one of each piece from the decorator fabric, matching the fabric design across seams, if necessary. Transfer all markings.

2. Staystitch the lower corners of the front piece, pivoting at the dots. Clip up to, but not through, the stitched corner.

3. Stitch darts on the front corners of the chair seat. Trim the excess fabric ¼" (6 mm) from the stitching, and press the seam allowances open.

4. Pin the chair seat to the front, matching the dots and lower edges. Stitch ½" (1.3 cm) seam. Finish the seam allowances and press them open.

5. Pin the front/seat to the back at the sides and top. Stitch. Using a ½" (1.3 cm) seam, stitch the chair front and back together across the top and down the sides. Finish the seam allowances and press them open.

6. If welting is desired, cut bias strips 1⅝" (4 cm) wide. The length of the welting is equal to the circumference of the lower edge of the slipcover. Make and apply welting as on page 184.

7. Measure the lower edge of the slipcover between the front darts. Add 14" (35.5 cm) for seam and pleat allowances to determine the width of the front skirt piece. Repeat for the sides, measuring from the dart to the side seam. Repeat for the back, measuring between side seams. To determine the length of the skirt pieces, double the measurement you recorded in step 8 of making the pattern, and add 1" (2.5 cm). At this length, the skirt will brush the floor. Adjust the measurement if you want it shorter. Cut the four skirt pieces.

8. Stitch the skirt pieces together into a circle, using ½" (1.3 cm) seams. Press the seam allowances open. Fold the skirt in half crosswise, wrong sides together. Baste the upper edges together within the ½" (1.3 cm) seam allowance.

9. Mark with pins 6½" (16.5 cm) on each side of one of the skirt seams. Fold the skirt at the pin marks and bring the folds to the seam to form an inverted box pleat. Pin the pleat in place. Repeat at the three remaining seams.

10. Check the fit of the skirt; adjust the sizes of the pleats if necessary. Baste across the tops of the pleats within the ½" (1.3 cm) seam allowance. Baste the skirt to the chair seat and back, right sides together. Place the slipcover on the chair and check the length of the skirt. Adjust if necessary. Stitch ½" (1.3 cm) seam. Finish the seam allowances together, and press them away from the skirt.

Office Task Chair

Office task chairs are meant for medium-duty use and are perfect for home and small offices. Most have upholstered seats and back, with many being adjustable for height. They are very industrial looking and over time can become dirty and worn. A fabric slipcover is just the thing to transform an ordinary office task chair into an inviting perch that will really dress up the space. The fabric choice, slipcover skirt style, and finishing details can be tailored to fit the office décor plus suit the people who use it.

YOU WILL NEED

- 2½ to 3 yd (2.3 to 2.75 m) of main fabric depending on repeat (for main body)

- 1 yd (0.92 m) of coordinating fabric (for cording and insert)

- cording for welting

- 2 yd (1.85 m) ribbon for bow-tie back closure

- Velcro

WHAT YOU NEED TO KNOW

This slipcover is made in two pieces to allow for adjusting the height of the chair back. Contrasting fabric used for an inverted box pleat in the back also makes it easier to slip the cover on and off. The contrasting fabric is repeated in the welting that outlines the seat and inside of the back. The seat cover is held in place with Velcro around the back post and underneath the seat from front to back.

If using decorator fabric with a large motif, for best results center the pattern on the seat, front skirt, and inside back. On the outside back, plan the seam to match the pattern at the top and align down the back when the pleat is closed.

If you want the cover to be washable, prewash and iron all of the fabric before cutting.

Measure and Mark Seat and Inside Back

1. Measure around the seat and inside back circumference to determine the total length of welting needed. Cut enough bias strips and stitch them together. Cover the cording. (See page 184.)

2. Measure the seat and inside back in both directions; record your measurements. Using pins, mark the center sides, top, and bottom of the back. Mark the center sides, front, and back of the seat.

Seat Slipcover Pattern

1. Cut a piece of fabric for the top of the seat, centering any design motif and allowing at least 1" (2.5 cm) extra in all directions. Place fabric on the chair seat. Beginning at center back, outline the seat with the welting, pinning it in place onto the decorator fabric with the lip extending downward. Allow enough welting to overlap the ends.

2. Stitch the welting to the seat fabric, overlapping the ends (page 184). Trim excess fabric.

3. Mark the seat corners for placement of inverted box pleats. Measure the front between the marks. Mark the seat back on either side of the back post. Measure the sides from the back mark to the pleat.

4. Cut three 7¼" (18.4 cm) strips for the skirt; this allows for a 6" (15.2 cm) skirt with ½" (1.3 cm) seam allowance at the top and ¾" (2 cm) single-fold hem at the bottom. Cut the front piece 6" (15 cm) wider than the measurement between pleats. Cut the sides 10½" (26.8 cm) wider than the measurement from pleat to back mark. These measurements allow for seam allowances inside the pleats and single-fold hems at the back.

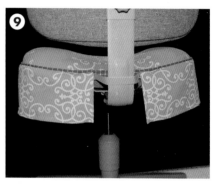

5. Sew the skirt pieces together. Finish the lower edge, then turn up ¾" (2 cm) hem and stitch. Finish the ends, then turn under ¾" (2 cm) hems and stitch. Fold box pleats at the front corners; press. Baste across the tops of the pleats.

6. With right sides together, pin the skirt to the seat, matching the pleat centers to the marks and the hemmed ends to the back marks. Sew the skirt to the seat.

7. Place the cover on the seat. Mark for placement of two Velcro straps to connect underneath the seat from front to back, one on each side of the center post.

8. Sew the Velcro straps in place.

9. Sew two shorter straps of Velcro to wrap around back post.

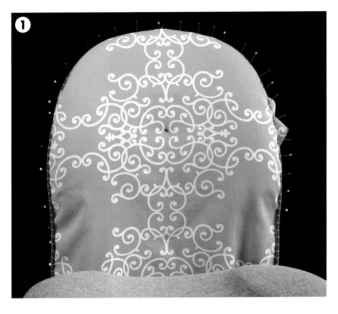

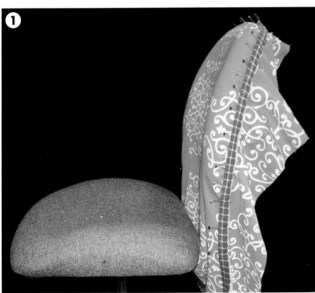

Back Slipcover

1. Cut a piece of fabric for the inside of the back, centering any design motif and allowing at least 1" (2.5 cm) extra at the sides and top and extending at least ¾" (2 cm) beyond the bottom of the seat skirt. Place fabric on the inside back; anchor with pins. Beginning at one lower edge, outline the inside back with the welting, pinning it in place onto the decorator fabric with the lip extending toward the back.

2. Stitch the welting to the inside back fabric. Trim excess fabric.

3. Place the cover on the back, mark with a pin where the fabric meets the back post as it goes under the seat. Draw a curved cut-out area to clear the back post.

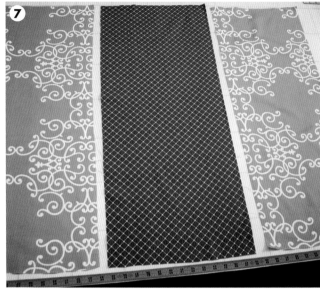

4. Cut out the back post area. Serge/finish the edge of cutout.

5. Turn under ½" (1.3 cm) hem and topstitch around the cutout.

6. Measure the outside back, allowing ample length to match skirt length (plus hem and seam allowance). Measure the outside back width; divide by 2 and add 2" (5 cm). Cut two pieces of fabric to these measurements. If using a print, take care to cut the pieces so the print will align at the center ½" (1.3 cm) seam line.

7. Cut the pleat center from contrasting fabric 14" (35.5 cm) wide and the same length as the main fabric pieces. Sew the outside back pieces together.

(continued)

8. Fold the outside back in half, right sides together. Stitch from the top down about 5" (12.8 cm) along the seams, matching the design, if any.

9. Press the pleat in place and baste across the top of the pleat.

Matching Patterns

It is usually impossible to match a fabric pattern across all the seams in a slipcover. Match the pattern in the areas that are most visible, such as the seam between the seat and chair back and the seam between the seat front and the skirt front.

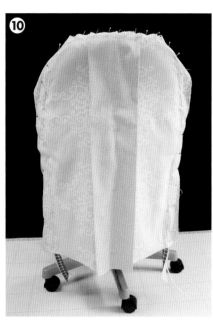

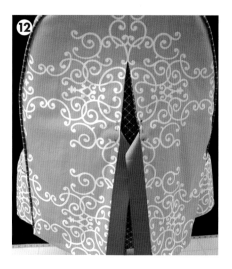

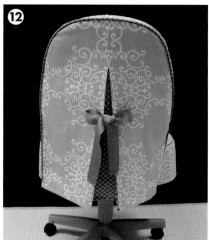

10. Place the inside back and outside back on the chair, wrong sides out. Pin the outer edges together, shaping the cover to fit the chair. Remove the cover and sew the pieces together.

11. Replace the cover on the chair. Mark the lower edge even with the skirt hem. Trim excess length to ¾" (2 cm). Finish the lower edge, then turn up ¾" (2 cm) hem and stitch.

12. Cut two 1-yd (0.92 m) ribbons for tie. Finish one end of each ribbon with a narrow double-fold hem. Turn under the opposite ends and stitch the ribbons opposite each other to the underside of the back pleat.

Resin Lawn Chair

You can transform a stacking resin chair with a loose-fitting slipcover made of indoor/outdoor decorator fabric. These inexpensive lawn chairs come in a variety of shapes and sizes. Fabric slipcovers dress them up for special occasions or for everyday use on your patio or deck. No one will guess what's under the cover!

YOU WILL NEED

- muslin for making patterns
- indoor/outdoor decorator fabric
- twill tape or grosgrain ribbon

WHAT YOU NEED TO KNOW

This slipcover consists of four pieces: one piece that wraps around the outside, covering the back and arms; one piece that wraps around the inside, covering the back and arms; one seat piece; and a gathered skirt. The inner and outer pieces are placed with the lengthwise grain running horizontally. They can usually be cut from one width of 54" (137 cm) fabric. To ensure the slipcover fits well, the pattern is pin-fitted with muslin.

Pin-fitting the Pattern

1. Mark the center of the chair at the top of the back and at the front and back of the seat with tape. Measure the chair from the front of one arm, around the back, to the front of the other arm (1). Then measure from the top of the back to a few inches below the seat (2). Add 6" (15 cm) in both directions and cut muslin to size. Using a permanent marker, mark a vertical line at the center back, and mark the lengthwise grain line of the pattern piece.

2. Measure the inside of the chair from the front of one arm, across the back, to the front of the other arm (3). Then measure from the top of the back to the top of the seat (4). Add 6" (15 cm) in both directions and cut muslin to size. Mark a vertical line at the center back. Mark the lengthwise grain of the pattern piece.

(continued)

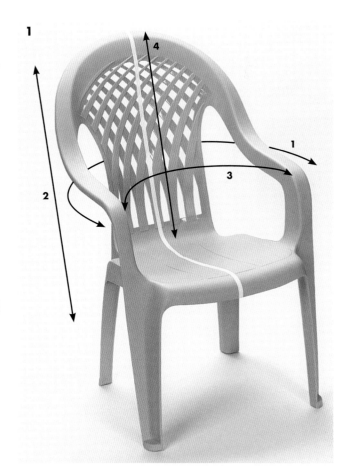

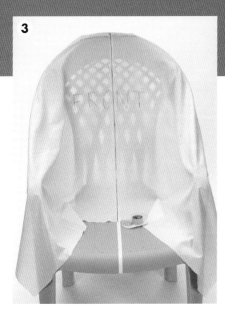

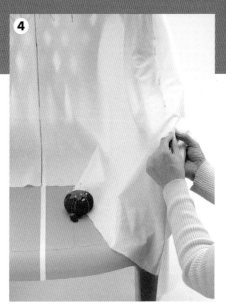

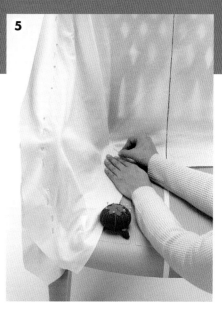

3. Pin the inner and outer patterns together at the center back line. Drape the pinned pattern over the chair, matching the center back lines to the center of the chair. Smooth the inner pattern down over the inner back of the chair, keeping the marked line in the center of the chair. Using double-stick tape, secure the inner pattern to the chair seat at the base of the center line and at the back corners of the seat.

4. Drape the outer pattern around the curve of the chair to the front of the arms, keeping the side grain lines perpendicular to the floor. Pin the inner and outer patterns together along the edge of the chair back and arms. Trim away some of the excess fabric over the arms to make this step easier. At the front of the arms, pin the patterns together in a straight line to the outer front corner of the seat, rather than fitting it to the

shape of the arms. Keep the grain lines perpendicular to the floor.

5. Pin excess fullness of the inner pattern into two pleats at the back corners of the seat so the pattern fits as smoothly as possible.

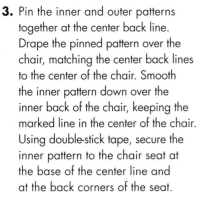

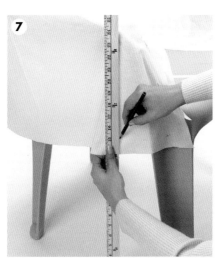

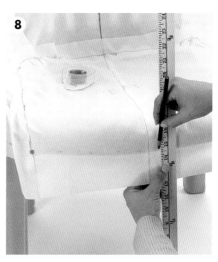

6. Mark the lower edge of the inner pattern along the outer edge of the seat. Mark a point at each front top corner where the upper and inner covers meet. Trim the pattern to 1" (2.5 cm) beyond the marked line.

7. Measure the distance from the floor to the lower edge of the seat front. Mark a line on the outer pattern the same distance from the floor. Trim the pattern to 1" (2.5 cm) beyond the marked line.

8. Cut muslin a few inches larger than the chair seat, extending down past the lower edge of the seat front. Mark a center line. Secure the pattern to the chair seat with double-stick tape, aligning the centers.

Pin the seat piece to the inner back pattern where it aligns to the marked line on the inner pattern. Mark the front of the seat even with the lower edge of the outer pattern. Mark the points where the inner and upper back pieces meet (marked in step 6). Mark the position of the box pleats at the back corners. Trim the seat pattern to 1" (2.5 cm) beyond the marked line.

9. Adjust the fit. Mark all the pinned seam lines and the pleats. Mark points where seams intersect and any other points that will be helpful when stitching the slipcover together.

10. Remove the pattern from the chair. Remove the pins. Cut the pattern pieces ½" (1.3 cm) beyond marked seam lines. Fold each piece in half to check for symmetry and adjust the seam lines if necessary. Use the pattern pieces to cut out the decorator fabric. Transfer all marks. For the slipcover skirt, measure from the lower edge of the seat front (same measurement taken in step 7) and add 2½" (6.5 cm) for seam and hem allowances. Cut two strips equal to this measurement across the width of the decorator fabric and trim the selvages.

Sewing the Slipcover

1. Staystitch the lower edge of the inner back piece a scant ½" (1.3 cm) from the edge. Fold the pleats at the marks and baste in place. Pin the upper edges of the inner and outer back pieces, right sides together, matching marks. Stitch a ½" (1.3 cm) seam.

2. Pin the seat to the lower edge of the inner back, right sides together, aligning the pleats to the marks at the back corners. Clip the seam allowance of the inner back as necessary to allow it to fit around the curves of the seat. The lower front edge of the seat will align to the lower edge of the outer slipcover. Stitch.

3. Sew the short ends of the skirt strips right sides together and press the seams open. Finish one long edge with serging or zigzag stitches. Press under 1½" (3.8 cm) and topstitch the hem in place.

4. Pin-mark the raw edge of the skirt in fourths. Between each set of pin marks, stitch two rows of gathering threads. Also pin-mark the lower edge of the slipcover in fourths.

5. Pin the skirt to the slipcover, right sides together, matching pin marks. Pull each set of gathering threads to evenly gather the skirt to fit the cover; knot the thread ends to secure. Stitch the skirt in place and press.

6. Cut two 24" (61 cm) lengths of twill tape or ribbon. Fold the strips in half and stitch one securely to the seam allowances on the underside of the slipcover at each seat back corner.

7. Put the slipcover on the chair. Lift the skirt and tie the twill-tape ties to the back chair legs to hold the slipcover in place.

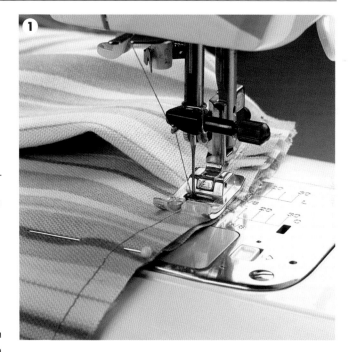

Outdoor Furniture

Custom-fitted cushions will make your chairs and chaise lounges comfortable and stylish. These soft cushions are filled with layers of polyester upholstery batting and covered with the indoor/outdoor fabric of your choice. The cushions are sewn with a simple mock-box construction that requires only front and back pieces (no separate sides). Stitching lines across the cushions allow them to bend and conform to the shape of the furniture. Stitching lines can also be used to create a head or leg rest.

YOU WILL NEED

- indoor/outdoor decorator fabric
- polyester upholstery batting or preexisting chaise cushions
- aerosol adhesive for polyurethane foam

WHAT YOU NEED TO KNOW

Depending on the style of furniture, cushions can be secured with ties or a hood. Plan ahead before you start the project. Ties can be secured around the frame of many metal and wooden furniture pieces and are sometimes inserted through the openwork of a mesh deck or between straps, bars, or slats. For a cushion that is reversible, stitch the ties at the side seams. If the furniture does not have any open areas for ties, create a hood to fit over the back. How-to steps for a hood or ties follow later in the project. (See photos below.)

Instead of layering polyester upholstery batting, you can cut pieces of indoor/outdoor cushion insert material, such as NU-Foam by Fairfield. This polyester product acts like foam but is treated to resist mildew and it will not disintegrate or lose its shape.

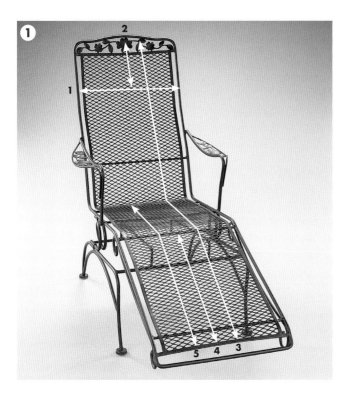

Cushions with Rounded Corners

1. Measure the width of the chair or chaise from side to side (1). Measure the distance from the top of the frame to the desired depth of the headrest (2). Measure the length of the chair or chaise lounge frame from the top of the back to the front of the frame (3). Measure the distance from the front edge to the back of the seat (4); if the chaise lounge has a curved or bent leg rest area, also measure the depth of the leg rest from the front edge to the highest point on the frame (5). Record the measurements.

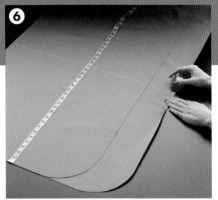

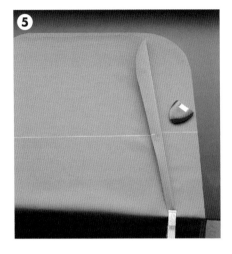

7. Cut and attach the hood piece, if desired. Place the front and back cushion pieces right sides together; pin, matching the marks on the sides.

8. Machine-stitch ½" (1.3 cm) from the raw edges, starting on one long side, just beyond the rounded corner; stitch across the end, down the opposite long side, across the opposite end, and stop just beyond the last corner.

(continued)

2. Add 4" (10 cm) to the length and width to allow for seam allowances and the thickness of the cushion. In addition, add 2" (5 cm) to the length for each stitching line across the cushion. Cut two pieces of fabric to this size.

3. Trace the upper and lower curved corners of the frame on paper. Trim the paper along the curved lines.

4. Place the pattern for the curves at the corners of the layered fabric, with the marked lines tapering to the raw edges at the top and sides; pin in place. Trim the fabric along the curves.

5. Measure from the upper edge of the fabric a distance equal to the desired depth of the headrest plus 3" (7.5 cm). Using chalk, mark a line on the right side of each piece across the width. Mark the ends of the lines on the wrong sides.

6. **For a chair or chaise with a leg extension,** measure from the lower edge of the fabric a distance equal to the measurement from the front of the frame to the back of the seat plus 3" (7.5 cm). Using chalk, mark a line across the right side of each piece. Mark the ends of the lines on the wrong sides of the fabric pieces.

For a chaise lounge with a bent leg rest, measure from the lower edge of the fabric a distance equal to the depth of the leg rest plus 3" (7.5 cm); mark a chalk line on the right side of each piece across the width. Also measure from the lower edge of the fabric a distance equal to the measurement from the front of the frame to the back of the seat plus 5" (12.8 cm); mark a chalk line on the right side of each fabric piece. Mark the ends of both lines on the wrong sides of the pieces.

9. Stitch ½" (1.3 cm) from the raw edges on the remaining long side, starting and stopping 2" (5 cm) from each marked line; this leaves an opening in each section of the cushion. Clip the seam allowances of the rounded corners.

10. Turn the cover right-side out through one opening. Make and position the ties, if desired (page 47). On the sides of the cushion, fold 1" (2.5 cm) inverted tucks at the stitching lines as shown and pin in place; enclose the ties, if any, in the tucks. Pin the front and back cushion pieces together along the stitching lines.

11. Stitch along the marked stitching lines, stitching the tucks in place at the sides. If the cushion has ties, catch the ties in the stitching of the tucks.

12. Cut four pieces of polyester upholstery batting for the area at the top of the cushion, cutting the pieces 1" (2.5 cm) wider than the chair or chaise lounge frame and 1" (2.5 cm) longer than the depth of the headrest; round the corners. Stack and secure two pieces of batting together, applying aerosol adhesive to both inner sides. Repeat to secure all four layers.

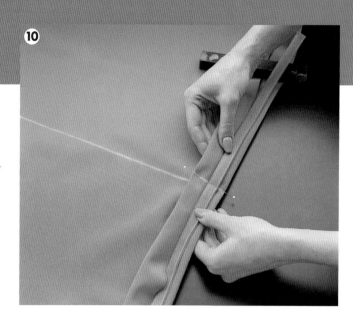

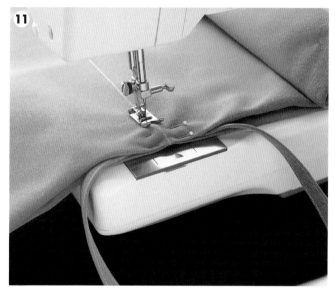

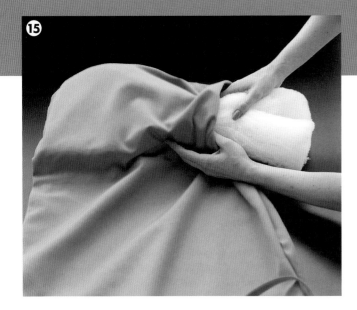

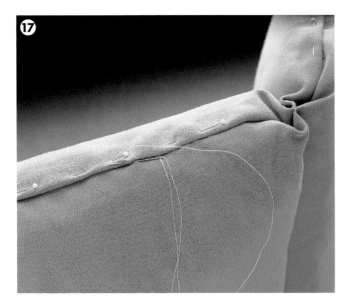

13. Repeat step 12 for the section at the bottom of the cushion, using four pieces of batting 1" (2.5 cm) wider than the frame and 1" (2.5 cm) longer than the measurement from the front of the frame to the back of the seat. If you're making a cushion for a chaise lounge with a leg rest, use pieces 1" (2.5 cm) longer than the depth of the leg rest.

14. Repeat step 12 for the middle section or sections of the cushion, using pieces of batting 1" (2.5 cm) wider than the frame, with the length of each piece equal to the distance between the stitching lines minus 1" (2.5 cm).

15. Fold the layered batting for the headrest in half crosswise; insert it into the headrest area through the opening, pulling the batting all the way to the opposite side of the cushion. Unfold the batting and smooth it in place. Adjust the position of the batting as needed, filling the corners with pieces of batting, if necessary.

16. Repeat step 15 for the remaining areas of the cushion, using corresponding sections of the batting.

17. Pin the openings on the side of the cushion closed; slipstitch.

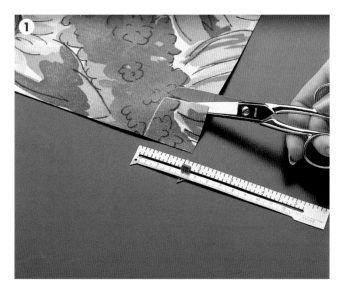

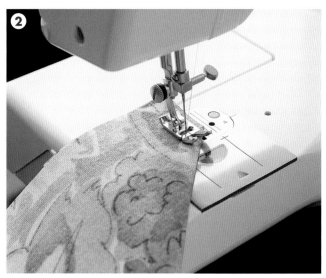

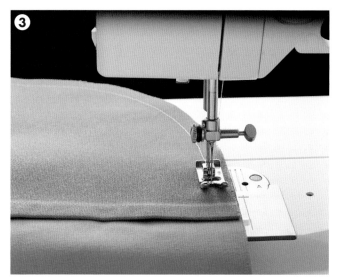

Cushions with Square Corners

1. Measure the chair or chaise frame and cut the fabric as in steps 1 and 2 (pages 42 and 43). At the corners, use chalk to mark a 1½" (3.8 cm) square; cut on the marked lines.

2. Fold the corners, matching the raw edges; stitch a ½" (1.3 cm) seam, 2" (5 cm) long, as shown. Complete the cushion by folding the corner seam allowances of the front and back pieces in opposite directions to distribute the bulk.

Hooded Back

1. Cut the fabric for the hood piece, 4" (10 cm) wider than the chair or lounge frame and 8½" (21.3 cm) long. For a cushion with rounded corners, trim the upper corners of the hood, using the pattern from step 3 for cushions with rounded corners (page 43).

2. On the lower edge of the hood piece, make a ½" (1.3 cm) double-fold hem.

3. Pin the hood to the cushion back, right sides up; baste near the edges. Complete the cushion as shown.

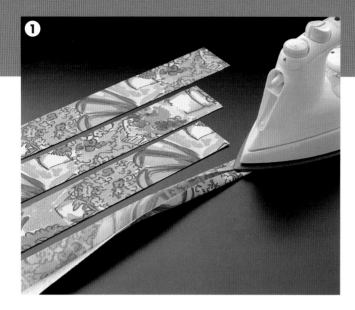

Ties

1. Cut four 2" x 24" (5 cm x 61 cm) strips of fabric for the ties. Press them in half lengthwise, wrong sides together; unfold. Fold the raw edges to the center; press.

2. Refold the ties in half, enclosing the raw edges. Edgestitch close to both long edges of the ties.

3. Pin the ties to the sides of the cushion at the marked stitching lines for the headrest and back of the seat. Complete the cushion as in steps 10 to 17 for cushions with rounded corners.

Ottomans

Rectangular ottomans with attached cushions are often used with upholstered chairs and sofas. Their styling is so basic that they easily blend with various furniture styles. This slipcover features a tailored skirt with inverted box pleats at the corners.

WHAT YOU NEED TO KNOW

This skirted slipcover is suitable for an ottoman that has short legs or bun feet, with or without a skirt. Pin-fitting with muslin isn't necessary because all the pieces are rectangular and easily measured with a tape measure. The top and boxing strip are welted in the same dimensions as the ottoman itself. A hidden lip of fabric that extends from the boxing strip under the skirt helps you pull the cover firmly into place. Twill-tape ties sewn to this lip are tied around the legs to keep the slipcover from sliding up. The skirt is lined for body and to avoid a noticeable hem around the bottom.

Cutting Directions

1. Measure the top of the ottoman from seam to seam. Add 1" (2.5 cm) in both directions for seam allowances, and cut a rectangle of fabric for the slipcover top.

2. Measure the width of the ottoman boxing strip from seam to seam. Add ½" (1.3 cm) for the upper seam allowance and 1½" (3.8 cm) for the lower extension. The finished length of the slipcover boxing strip equals the circumference of the ottoman. You will have to seam the boxing strip in two equal pieces, so divide this measurement in half and add 1" (2.5 cm) for seam allowances. Cut the boxing strip pieces on the crosswise grain of the fabric, matching the print to one side of the slipcover top, if necessary.

3. Measure for the skirt length from the lower seam of the ottoman boxing strip to the floor. (If the ottoman usually stands on carpet, measure on carpet for accuracy.) Add 2½" (6.5 cm) to this measurement for the cut length of the skirt. Cut four skirt pieces, one for each side, with the widths equal to the cut sides of the ottoman top plus 16" (40.5 cm).

4. Cut lining pieces the same widths as the skirt pieces and 2" (5 cm) shorter than the skirt pieces.

5. Cut bias fabric strips for the welting (page 186) with the length equal to twice the circumference of the ottoman plus additional length for seaming strips, joining ends, and inconspicuously positioning seams.

Sewing the Slipcover

1. Make welting as on page 184. Stitch the welting around the outer edge of the slipcover top, following the continuous circle method.

2. Sew the boxing strip pieces together with ½" (1.3 cm) seams. Finish the lower edge of the boxing strip with zigzag stitches or serging. Pin the boxing strip to the slipcover top, matching the print on one side, if necessary. Clip into the boxing strip seam allowance at the corners to allow the fabric to spread. Stitch the boxing strip to the top, using a welting foot or zipper foot.

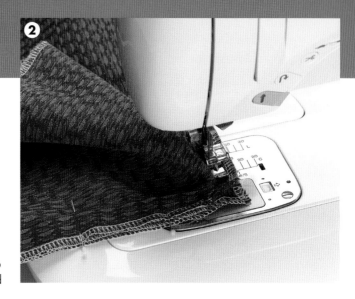

3. Mark a chalk line 1" (2.5 cm) from the lower edge of the boxing strip. Stitch the welting in a continuous circle to the boxing strip, aligning the raw edges of the welting to the marked line. Mark the lower edge of the boxing strip at the corners, even with the pivot points of the stitching on the top edge.

4. Sew the skirt pieces together in a big circle, using ½" (1.3 cm) seam allowances. Repeat for the lining pieces. Press the seam allowances open.

5. Pin the lower edges of the skirt and lining right sides together, matching seams. Stitch ½" (1.3 cm) from the edges. Press the seam allowances toward the lining.

6. Fold the lining and skirt, wrong sides together, aligning the upper edges. Press. Baste the upper edges together.

7. At the upper edge of the skirt, at each seam, place a pin 1" (2.5 cm) to the left of the seam, a second pin 7" (18 cm) to the right of the seam, and a third pin 15" (38 cm) to the right of the seam. Fold each pleat, bringing the outer pin marks to the center pin mark; pin them in place. The seams will be hidden in the folds of the pleats.

8. Check the skirt for fit, and adjust the folds if necessary. Baste across the top of each pleat.

9. Pin the upper edge of the skirt over the welting at the lower edge of the boxing strip, right sides together, aligning the raw edges and matching the marks on the boxing strip to the centers of the pleats. Stitch, using a welting foot or zipper foot.

10. To make the ties, cut eight lengths of twill tape, 18" (46 cm) long. Stitch the ties to the extension of the boxing strip, 2" (5 cm) from each corner.

11. Place the slipcover on the ottoman, pulling on the boxing strip extension to position it snugly in place. Tie the ties behind the ottoman legs to keep the slipcover in place.

Securing Option

If your ottoman has casters, very short feet, or no feet at all, ties are impractical. Secure the slipcover by inserting screw pins through the boxing strip extension into the upholstered sides of the ottoman.

Club Chair

A tightly fitting slipcover works well on fully upholstered armchairs like this club chair. The directions that follow are also useful for making fitted slipcovers for sofas. The styles are similar but with more cushions. A slipcover can be made from a single fabric or several coordinating fabrics. For interest and stability, add contrasting welting in the seams. Make the skirts tailored, box pleated, or gathered to suit your taste.

YOU WILL NEED

- muslin for making a pattern

- decorator fabric (see chart on page 180 for estimate)

- cording for welting

- zippers; one for chairs, two for sofas and love seats. The length of each zipper is 1" to 2" (2.5 to 5 cm) shorter than the length of the vertical seam at the side of the outside back. Additional zippers are needed for cushions (page 91).

WHAT YOU NEED TO KNOW

A common concern about slipcovers is whether or not they will stay in place. Precise construction of the slip-cover with proper seam placement is the key to making a great-looking slipcover. If this is done correctly on the right angels, there is no need to insert foam in the deck-ing or to pin the slipcover to the furniture.

Furniture with a concave back design, such as a chan-nel back or barrel back, can be more difficult to cover and may not fit as well. An undergarment of interlining or flannel cloth can be wrapped over the back before it is slipcovered. Furniture with a tufted back or with but-tons on the back can be slipcovered, but the tufting and buttons will be concealed by the slipcover. The back has to be wrapped with upholstery batting to fill it out for a smooth-fitting slipcover.

Making a Pattern for a Fitted Slipcover

One method for making a slipcover pattern is to pin-fit muslin on the chair or sofa. Before you start, look carefully at the furniture. Usually the seams in the slipcover will be in the same locations as the seams on the existing cover, but you may be able to add or eliminate some details, if it will not affect the fit of the slipcover. For example, if the existing cushions are waterfall style (wrapped in one piece from front to back), you can slipcover them as box cushions with welting. Or a chair with a pleated front arm can be slipcovered with a separate flat front arm piece.

The style of the skirt can also be changed. You may want to gather a skirt all the way around the furniture, allowing double fullness. Or you may want bunched gathers at the corners of a chair, or at the corners and center front of a sofa. For a more tailored look, the skirt can have box pleats instead of gathers.

A chair with rolled arms and loose back and seat cush-ions is used in the instructions that follow. This example includes the details that are common to most furniture. Although your furniture style may be different, use these basic steps as a guide.

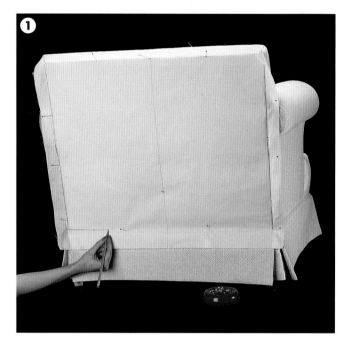

Pin-fitting the Pattern for the Back

1. Remove the cushions. Measure the outside back of your chair or sofa between seam lines; cut muslin 3" to 4" (7.5 to 10 cm) larger than measurements. Mark a center line on the outside back piece, following the lengthwise grain. Pin the muslin piece to the chair, smoothing fabric; mark seam lines.

2. Measure the inside back between seam lines; cut muslin 15" (38 cm) wider and about 10" (25.5 cm) longer than measurements. This allows for 6" (15 cm) at the lower edge to tuck into the deck and hold the slipcover in place. Mark a center line on the inside back piece, following lengthwise grain.

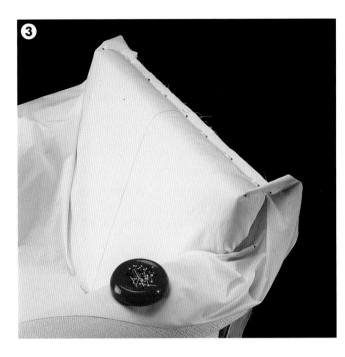

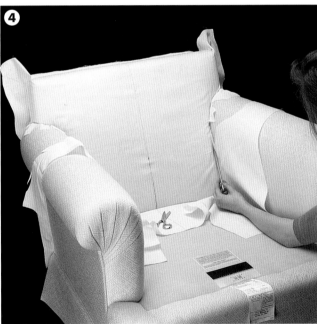

3. Pin the outside back and inside back together along the top of the chair or sofa, matching center lines. Fold out excess fabric on the inside back piece at upper corner, forming a dart. Pin the muslin snugly, but do not pull the fabric tight.

4. Trim excess fabric on sides of the inside back to 2" (5 cm); clip along the arms as necessary for smooth curve. Push about ½" (1.3 cm) of fabric into crevices on sides and lower edge of the inside back; mark seam lines by pushing a pencil into crevices.

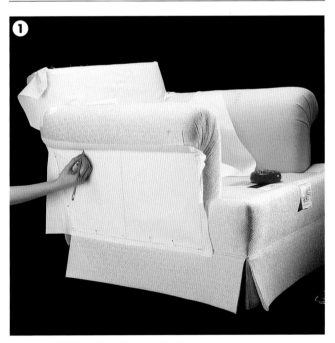

Pin-fitting the Pattern for a Pleated Arm

1. Measure the outside arm between seam lines; cut muslin 3" (7.5 cm) larger than measurements. Mark lengthwise grain line on the muslin. Pin the outside arm in place, with the grain line perpendicular to the floor and lower edge extending ½" (1.3 cm) beyond the seam line at the upper edge of the skirt. Smooth the fabric upward; pin. Pin the outside arm to the outside back. Mark the seam lines.

(continued)

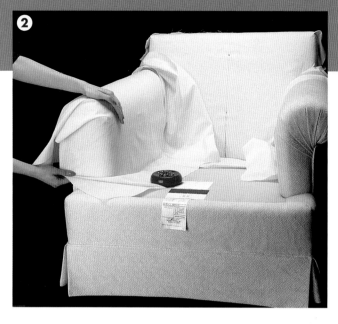

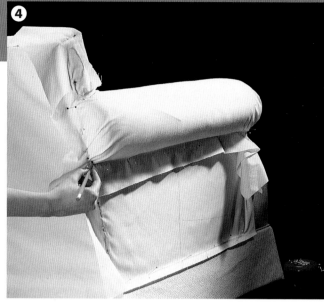

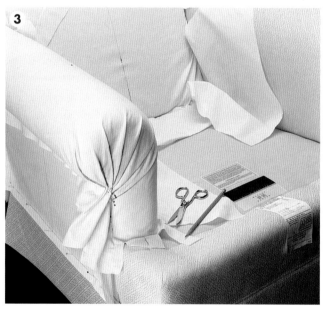

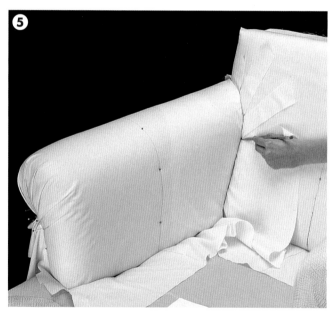

2. Measure the inside arm from deck to seam line at the upper edge of the outside arm, and from the inside back to the front of the arm; cut muslin about 9" (23 cm) larger than measurements. Mark lengthwise grain line on the muslin. Pin the inside arm piece in place, with 7" (18 cm) extending at inside back and grain line straight across the arm, smoothing fabric up and around the arm.

3. Pin the inside arm to the outside arm at front; clip and trim fabric at the front lower edge as necessary for a smooth fit. Pleat out fabric for the rolled arm to duplicate pleats in the existing fabric. Mark radiating fold lines of pleats.

4. Make tucks on the inside arm at the back of the chair, to fold out excess fabric; clip the inside arm as necessary for a smooth fit. Mark seam line at beginning and end of tucks on the inside arm and outside back.

5. Mark the inside arm and inside back with large dots, about halfway up the arm. Push about ½" (1.3 cm) of fabric on the inside arm into crevices at the deck and back.

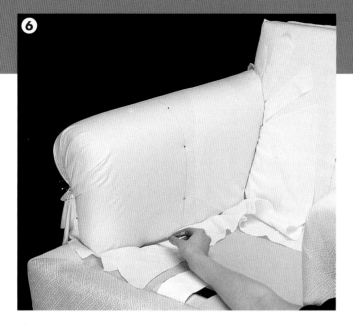

6. Mark all seam lines on the muslin, smoothing fabric as you go.

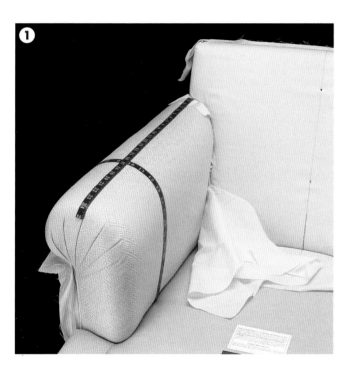

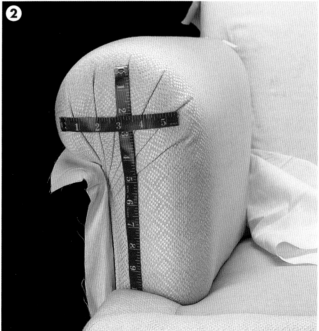

Pin-fitting the Pattern for an Arm with a Front Section

1. Follow page 55, step 1, for outside arm. Measure the inside arm from deck to seam line at the upper edge of the outside arm, and from the inside back to the front edge of the arm; cut muslin about 9" (23 cm) larger than these measurements. Mark lengthwise grain line on the muslin.

2. Measure front of the arm; cut muslin 2" to 3" (5 to 7.5 cm) larger than measurements. Mark lengthwise grain line on the muslin.

(continued)

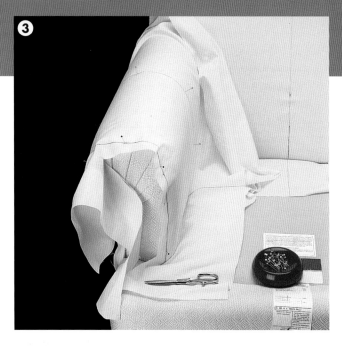

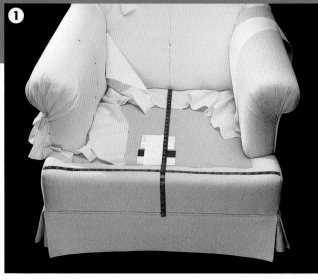

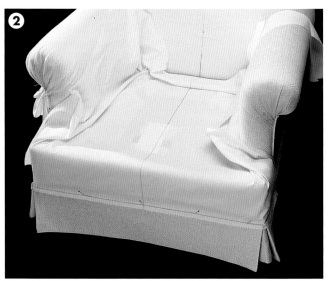

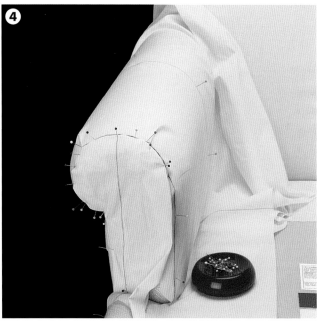

3. Pin the inside arm piece in place, with 7" (18 cm) extending at the inside back and grain line straight across the arm, smoothing fabric up and around the arm. Mark seam line at front edge of the arm; trim away excess fabric not needed for seam allowances.

4. Pin the front arm piece in place. Fold out excess fabric on the inside arm as necessary to fit the front arm piece, making two pleats. Mark seam line for the curve of the arm, following existing seam line on the chair. Complete the pattern as on pages 56 and 57, following steps 4, 5, and 6.

Pin-fitting the Pattern for the Deck

1. Measure the width at the deck front; measure the deck length, down the front of the chair to the skirt seam; cut muslin about 15" (38 cm) wider and 9" (23 cm) longer than these measurements. Mark a center line on the muslin, following the grain. Mark a seam line on the muslin at front edge on straight grain, ½" (1.3 cm) from the raw edge.

2. Pin the marked line on the muslin to the welting of the skirt seam, aligning the center line with the center of the skirt. Smooth muslin over the front edge and deck, and match center lines of deck and back.

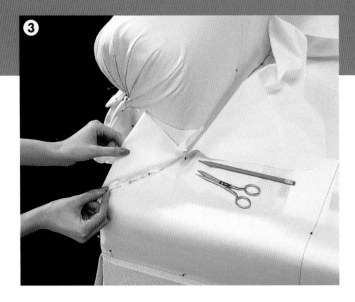

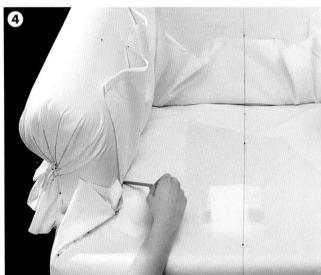

1. Measure for skirt around the sides, front, and back to determine the cut width of the skirt; allow for gathers or pleats. Plan seam placement based on width of fabric and size of the furniture, so seams are concealed in gathers or pleats whenever possible; plan a seam at the back corner where the zipper will be inserted. Cut the number of fabric widths needed; cut muslin pieces 1" (2.5 cm) longer than the length of the skirt.

2. Place raw edge of the muslin just below the lower edge of the skirt; pin at upper edge of the skirt, keeping muslin straight and even. Pin seams as you come to them; pin out fullness for pleats or gathers. Pin vertical tucks in the skirt, pinning ⅛" (3 mm) tuck near back corner on each side of the chair and ¼" (6 mm) tuck near each corner on back of the chair; tucks will be released in step 3 on page 60, adding ease to the skirt. Mark seams and placement of pleats or gathers.

3. Mark the deck and inside arm pieces with large dots, at the point where the deck meets the front of the inside arm. For furniture with a T-cushion, clip excess fabric to the dots. Fold out excess fabric on deck at the front corner, forming a dart; pin and mark.

4. Pin the deck to the outside arm piece at the side of the chair; mark the seam line. Do not fit the deck snug. Push about ½" (1.3 cm) of fabric into the crevices at the sides and back of the deck; mark seam lines by pushing a pencil into the crevices.

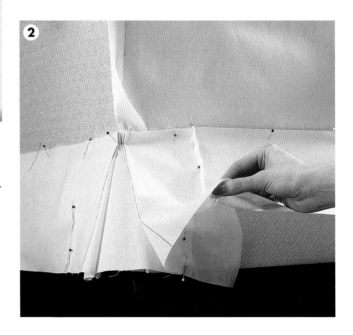

Attention to Grain Lines

Keep the grain lines of the pattern pieces parallel or perpendicular to the floor to ensure proper fit of the slipcover and make it easier to match designs at seams.

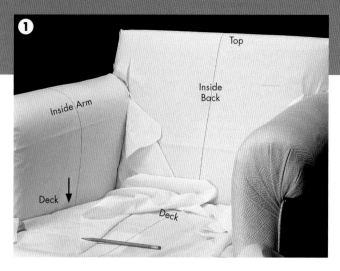

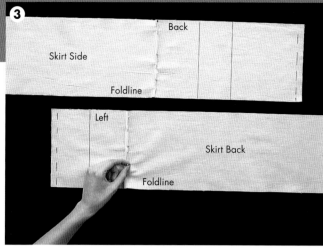

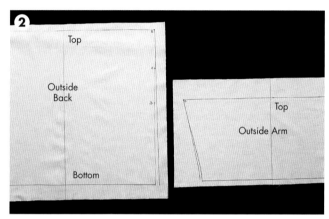

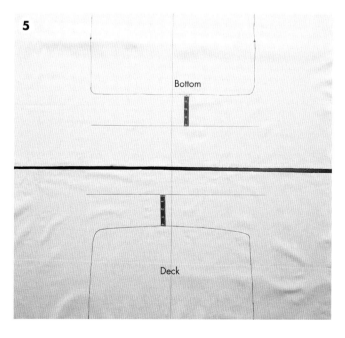

Preparing the Pattern for Cutting

1. Mark upper edge of all muslin pieces; label pieces. Check that all seam lines, darts, gathers, and pleats are marked. Mark dots at intersecting seams; label.

2. Remove the muslin. Add ¼" (6 mm) ease to back edge of the outside arm at lower corner. Add ½" (1.3 cm) ease to sides of the outside back at lower corners. Taper to the marked seam lines at upper corners.

3. Remove the pinned tucks near back corners of skirt pieces. Mark "fold line" at lower edge of the muslin for a self-lined skirt.

4. True straight seam lines, using a straightedge; true curved seam lines, drawing smooth curves. Do not mark seam lines in pleated areas.

5. Add 4" (10 cm) to lower edge of the inside back and back edge of deck.

6. Mark the lower edge of the inside arm from a point 4" (10 cm) away from seam line at the back edge to ½" (1.3 cm) from large dot at front edge; repeat for sides of the deck.

7. Mark back edge of the inside arm from a point 4" (10 cm) away from the seam line at the lower edge to ½" (1.3 cm) from the large dot; repeat for sides of the inside back.

8. Check lengths of the seam lines for adjoining seams; adjust as necessary to ensure that seam lines match.

9. Fold pleats on the marked lines. Mark seam lines in pleated area; add ½" (1.3 cm) seam allowances. Trim on cutting line through all layers of pleats. Add ½" (1.3 cm) seam allowances to any remaining seams. Cut pieces on the marked lines.

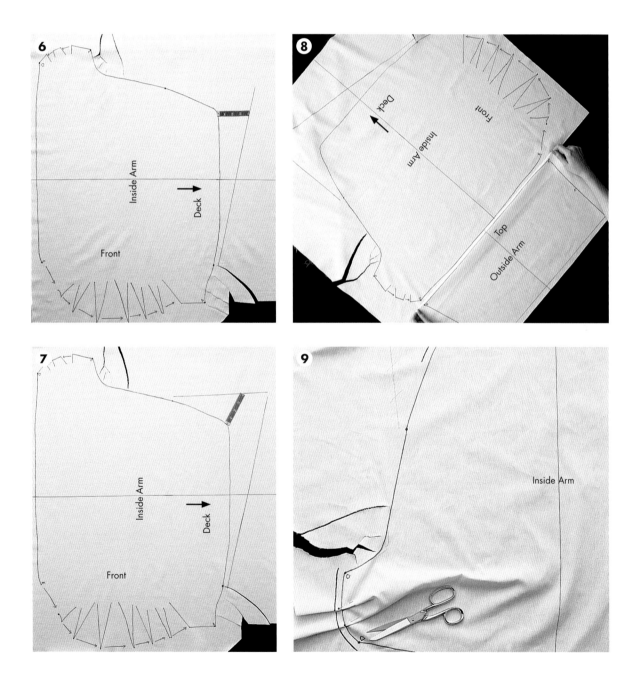

Cutting Directions

1. Cut out the pieces, following the general guidelines on page 181.

2. Cut a 3" (7.5 cm) tacking strip on the straight grain. This strip is used to secure the slipcover to the furniture with T-pins, tacks, or staples. Cut the length of the tacking strip equal to the distance around the furniture at the upper edge of the skirt.

Sewing the Fitted Slipcover

Although the slipcover for your furniture may be somewhat different from the style shown, many of the construction steps will be the same. It will be helpful to lay out the pieces and think through the sequence for sewing the seams of your slipcover. The labeled notches on adjoining seams will help you see how the pieces are to be joined together. To minimize handling of bulky quantities of fabric, stitch any small details, such as darts, before assembling the large pieces.

For durable seams, use a strong thread, such as long-staple polyester, and a medium stitch length of about 10 stitches per inch (2.5 cm). Because slipcovers have several thicknesses of fabric at intersecting seams with welting, use size 90/14 or 100/16 sewing needle.

Add welting to any seams that will be subjected to stress and wear, because welted seams are stronger than plain seams. For decorative detailing, welting can also be added to seams such as around the outside back and the upper edge of the skirt. On furniture with front arm pieces, welting is usually applied around the front of the arm as a design detail. See page 184 for instructions on making and applying welting.

For a chair, apply a zipper to one of the back seams of the slipcover. For a sofa, apply zippers to both back seams.

Sewing a Fitted Slipcover with a Pleated Front Arm

1. Stitch darts at the upper corners of the inside back. If welting is desired, apply it to the upper front edges of the outside arm, pivoting at the corner.

2. Stitch darts at the outer front corners of the deck; stop stitching ½" (1.3 cm) from the raw edges at the inner corner.

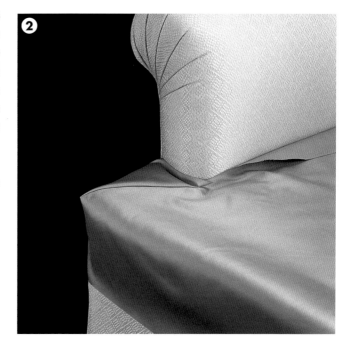

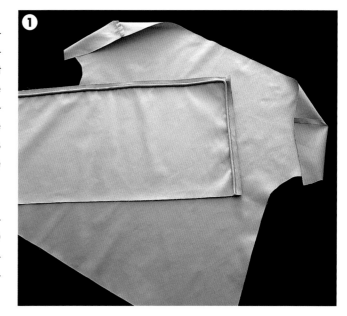

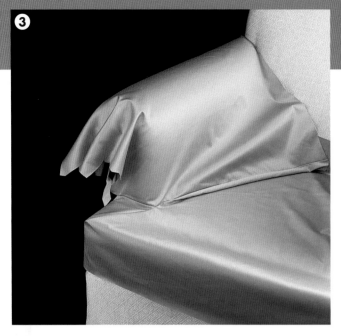

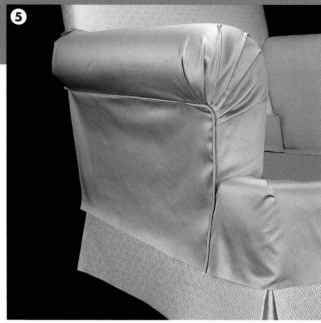

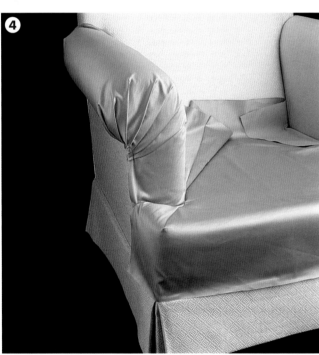

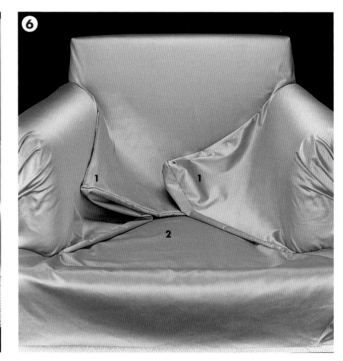

3. Stitch the deck to the front of the arm and the inside arm; this can be stitched as two separate seams.

4. Pin pleats in place at the front and back of the arm. Check the fit over the arm of the chair. Baste in place on seam line.

5. Stitch the horizontal and vertical seams, joining the outside arm to inside arm; pivot at corner.

6. Pin the inside arms to inside back on both sides (1). Pin lower edge of the inside back to back edge of the deck (2). Make tucks in seams at the corners if necessary so pieces fit together. Stitch seams.

(continued)

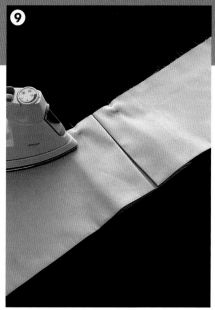

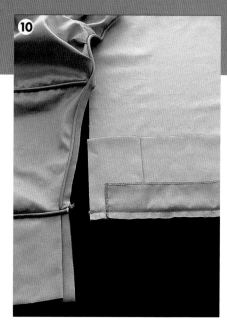

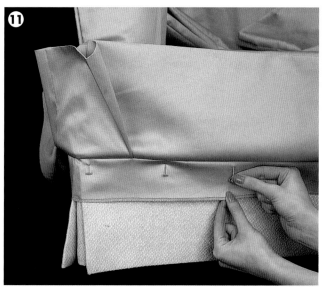

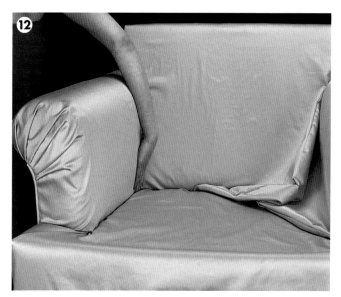

7. Apply welting around the sides and upper edge of slip-cover unit (page 184); curve ends of the welting into seam allowance ½" (1.3 cm) from the lower edges (arrow). Join slipcover unit to outside back, leaving seam open for zipper application. Apply welting to the lower edge.

8. Stitch skirt pieces together, leaving seam at the back corner unstitched for zipper insertion; press seams open. Fold the skirt in half lengthwise with wrong sides together; press.

9. Press pleats for pleated skirt. For a gathered skirt, stitch gathering stitches by zigzagging over a cord; for a skirt with bunched gathers, stitch gathering stitches between the markings.

10. Pin the tacking strip to the upper edge of the skirt on the wrong side. Join the skirt to adjoining pieces; for a gathered skirt, pull the gathering threads together to fit. Apply the zipper (page 66). Sew cushion covers (pages 91 to 99).

11. Apply slipcover to furniture. Secure the tacking strip to the furniture by pinning it into upholstery with T-pins.

12. Push extra fabric allowance into crevices around the deck and inside back. Stuff 2" (5 cm) strips of polyurethane foam into crevices around the deck to keep fabric from pulling out. Insert the cushions.

Sewing a Fitted Slipcover with a Front Arm Piece

1. Stitch darts at the upper corners of the inside back. Apply welting to the upper edge of the inside arm, if desired. Stitch the horizontal seam, joining the outside arm to the inside arm. Pin and baste tucks at the front edge of the inside/outside arm.

2. Stitch the front arm piece to the front edge of the inside/outside arm; stop stitching 2" (5 cm) from the outer end of the front arm piece.

3. Follow steps 2 and 3 on page 62 and 63. Pin the pleats in place at the back of the arm; baste in place on the seam line.

4. Complete the vertical seam at the front edge of the outside arm. Finish the slipcover as in steps 6 through 12 on pages 63 and 64.

Preshrink Materials

If you intend to launder your slipcover occasionally, preshrink the fabric and choose polyester cording for the welting. If you must use cotton cording, tie it in a loose coil, dip it in hot water, place it in a mesh laundry bag, and dry it in a dryer before sewing the welting.

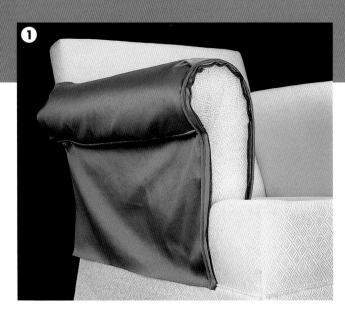

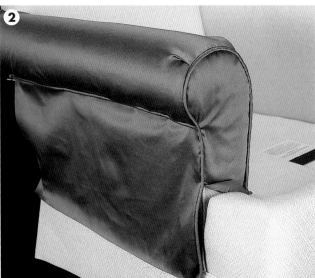

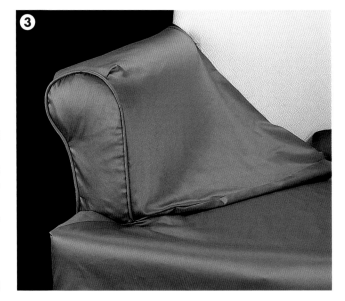

Applying the Zipper

1. Pull the cording out slightly from the ends of the skirt opening; trim off the ends 1" (2.5 cm). Pull the seam to return the cording to its original position.

2. Press under the seam allowances on the zipper opening. Place the open zipper on the welted side of the seam, so the welting just covers the zipper teeth and with the zipper tab at the lower edge. Pin in place; fold in the seam allowance at the lower edge of the skirt to miter. Fold up the end of the zipper tape.

3. Using a zipper foot, edgestitch on the skirt, with the zipper teeth positioned close to the folded edge. Stitch in the ditch of the welted seam.

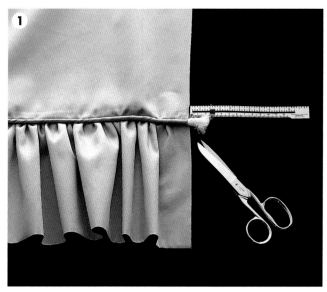

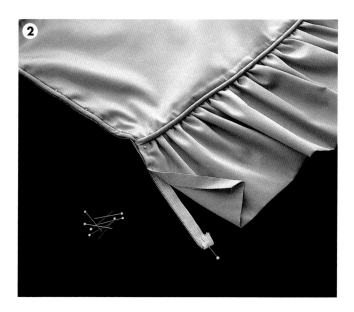

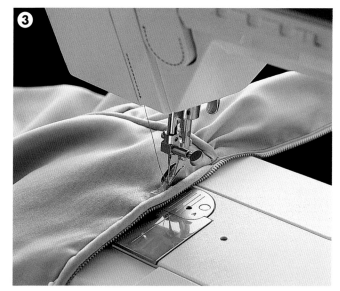

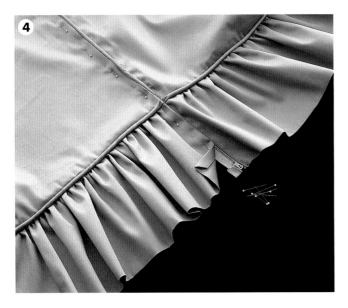

Pleated Skirt

1. Follow steps 1 through 5, opposite, except break the stitching at the upper edge of the skirt. On the skirt, stitch through the lower layer of the box pleat; stitch as close as possible to the seam at the upper edge of the skirt.

4. Close the zipper. Place the remaining side of the zipper under the seam allowance, with the folded edge at the welted seam line. Pin in place; fold in the seam allowance at the lower edge of the skirt to miter. Fold up the end of the zipper tape.

5. Open the zipper. Stitch ⅜" (1 cm) from the folded edge, pivoting at the top of the zipper.

Barrel Chair

Barrel or tub chairs, named for their distinctive curved backs, require darts or tucks at evenly placed areas on the inside back for a tailored fit. These chairs have a unique style that can really show off a funky fabric, not to mention the cozy barrel back is a comforting place to sit and relax.

YOU WILL NEED

- blue painter's tape
- approximately 9 yd (8.2 m) of decorator fabric
- topstitching thread
- measuring tape

WHAT YOU NEED TO KNOW

In the directions that follow, the decorator fabric is fitted directly onto the chair, rather than making a muslin pattern. For a chair with such a curvy shape, this direct method not only saves time but can also result in the best-fitting cover. Anchor the fabric pieces right-side out on the chair, keeping the cross grain parallel to the floor. After pin-fitting, trim the pieces, leaving uniform ½" (1.3 cm) seam allowances. Then remove the cover, disassemble, and repin right sides together for sewing.

The main slipcover is made in eight pieces: inside back (IB), two inside arms (IA), outside back (OB), two outside arms (OA), deck, and skirt. Seams in the slipcover will most likely correspond to seams in the upholstery, which will help when pin-fitting. The cushion for the chair shown is a waterfall style (page 91). However, if yours is a different style, refer to the instructions for that style when covering the cushion.

Welting was not used in the seams of this slipcover. For strength and to give the slipcover a more contemporary look, the seam allowances are pressed to one side and topstitched.

This particular chair swivels on an upholstered base, so a skirt was added at the bottom, falling straight down from just below the cushion. If your chair does not have this feature, you can still choose to have a skirt or make the slipcover go straight to the floor. If your chair curves inward at the bottom, avoid curving the slipcover inward or you will have difficulty getting it on the chair without inserting a zipper (page 66).

Because of the attractive curves, matching a large print on this chair is not possible. Made from this modern, medium-scale print, the slipcover is fun and interesting, and unmatched seams are not distracting.

Anchoring Fabric

1. Remove the cushion. Measure the inside back (IB) of the chair and mark the center with pins. If your slipcover will have a skirt, decide where you want the skirt to start and mark this distance evenly from the floor around the chair.

2. Leaving the roll of fabric on the floor behind the chair, pull the fabric up and over the back, centering the design by feeling for the pin marks under the fabric. Smooth the fabric down the IB. Cut the fabric at the deck, leaving about 6" (15 cm) for tuck-in allowance. Cut the sides of the IB, leaving about 8" (20 cm) beyond the upholstery seams for dart allowance. Anchor fabric on the IB with T-pins.

3. Smooth fabric down and away from the center. As excess fabric collects, pinch fabric on either side of the center motif, and pin the excess into darts. Sometimes, as in this example, the chair is not symmetrical; therefore the size of the darts will vary.

4. Continue to smooth fabric and pin darts in the entire IB.

5. Cut a piece of fabric for the deck, allowing 6" (15 cm) for tuck-in allowance and ample overhang at the front past the skirt seam marks. This will be tapered in a later step.

6. Cut fabric for an inside arm (IA), leaving allowances for tuck-in and pinning. Anchor the fabric to the chair, and smooth in place. Repeat for the other IA.

7. Cut a piece of fabric for the OB, centering the design and leaving ample allowance at the top to shape it to the curve of the chair. Leave 2" (5 cm) allowances at the sides (corresponding to upholstery seams) and lower edge (skirt seam). If there will not be a skirt, leave enough allowance at the floor to turn up a hem. Anchor OB to chair.

8. Cut fabric for the two OAs, leaving ample allowance at the top to shape it to the curve of the chair. Leave 2" (5 cm) allowances at the sides (corresponding to upholstery seams), front, and lower edge (skirt seam). If there will not be a skirt, leave enough allowance at the floor to turn up a hem. Anchor the OAs to the chair.

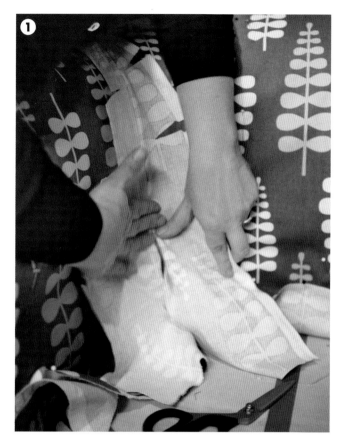

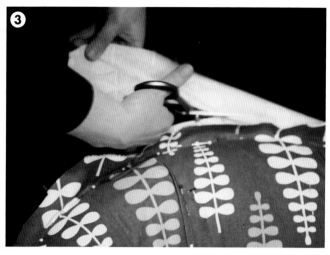

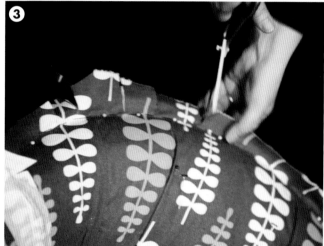

Pin-fitting

1. Pin IB to IAs, where they will be seamed together. Clip into the allowance as necessary to allow the fabric to lie smoothly.

2. Smooth IB over back of chair; smooth OB upward to meet the IB. Pin them together along the top, using the seam in the upholstery as a guide.

3. Trim excess seam allowances and clip as necessary to allow fabric to fit smoothly.

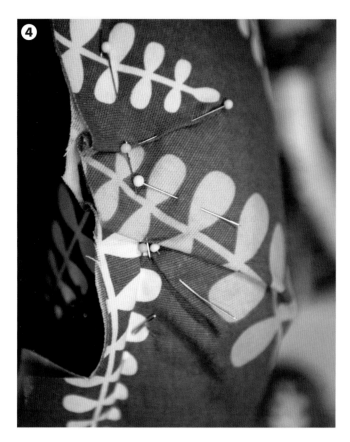

4

4. Smooth IAs outward and over the front. Pin tucks in the fabric as needed to shape the slipcover to the chair (an odd number of tucks is best). Then smooth the OAs upward to meet the IAs and pin along the seam line. Trim and clip the seam allowances.

5. Pin the deck to the IA at the front to fit the chair smoothly. Then pin the rest of the seam, gradually increasing the tuck-in depth toward the back to about 4" (10 cm). Repeat on the opposite side. Pin the back deck to the IB, allowing for 4" (10 cm) tuck-in.

6. When all pieces are smoothly pinned together, mark the skirt seam along the lower edge of the slipcover. Cut fabric for the skirt and pin it to the chair. Match the print at the front if possible. Pin inverted box pleats at the front corners and back, coinciding with the slipcover seams. Hide any seams inside the pleats. Allow 2" (5 cm) extra length: ½" (1.3 cm) for seam allowance and 1½" (3.8 cm) for hem.

7. Label all pieces with painter's masking tape. Remove anchor pins, then remove cover.

Preparing the Pieces

1. Mark the seam lines on the wrong side of the fabric, and trim the seam allowances to ½" (1.3 cm). Make notches and clip marks as necessary. Mark intersecting lines to help in matching seams. Remove pins from seams.

2. Mark darts in the IB and tucks in IAs pleats before removing pins.

3. Mark the pleats in the skirt.

Sewing the Slipcover

1. Pin the darts in the IB and stitch. Press all the darts away from the center. Topstitch ¼" (6 mm) away from the stitching lines. Pin the tucks in the front IAs, and baste across the ends to hold.

2. Pin the IAs to the IB. Stitch the seams. Serge/finish the seam allowances together, and press them away from the center. Topstitch ¼" (6 mm) away from the seam.

3. Pin the IA and IB to the deck, including lower front where it wraps around arms. Clip curved areas for ease, and then serge/finish seam allowances.

4. Join the OAs to the OB. Serge the seam allowances together and press them toward the center. Topstitch.

5. Pin the front to the back along the upper edge and arms. Stitch. Serge/finish the seam allowances together, and press them toward the front. Topstitch.

6. Stitch the skirt pieces together. Serge/finish the seams. Serge/finish the lower edge; turn up the hem and stitch. Fold the pleats in place and baste across the top. Sew the skirt to the slipcover.

Putting on the Cover

1. Starting from the top down, shimmy the cover onto the chair.

2. Smoothing down and out, arrange pleats in proper direction; begin to line up upper back seams.

3. With everything above the tuck-in area smoothed in place, start from center and work outward to push the tuck-in into place. Sometimes pushing down the deck with one hand while tucking will make this process easier.

4. Use an iron or steamer to help mold the fabric to the chair.

Cushion

1. Place the cushion on the chair. To help match the design so it flows uninterrupted from the IB to the cushion, lay a sheet of clear plastic over the cushion and up onto the chair back. Trace the back curve of the cushion and some identifying design motifs.

2. Place the plastic over the fabric and align the motif marks to the design in the fabric. Then cut a piece of fabric long enough to wrap from the back top around the cushion to the back bottom. Allow ample allowance for seams.

3. Wrap the fabric around the cushion. Pin out darts at the front if necessary to fit. Remove the fabric. Stitch the darts. Press the top darts down and the bottom darts up. Topstitch.

4. Follow the directions starting on page 91 to finish the cushion slipcover.

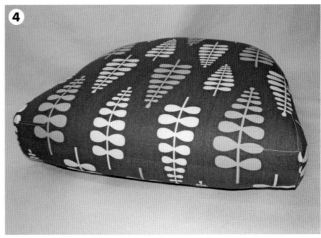

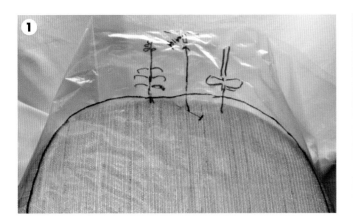

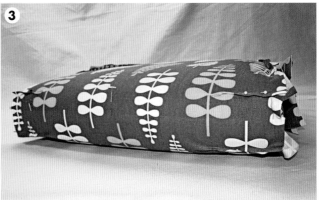

Snug Fit

If fabric is slippery or the tuck-in area is loose, stuff long pieces of foam in crevice to help keep back and deck in place.

THE COMPLETE PHOTO GUIDE TO SLIPCOVERS, PILLOWS & BEDDING

Open Arm Rocker

The retro styling of boomerang arms on this rocking chair called for a bold fabric to make it stand out and give it vibrant new character. With its mad, mod style, this fun orange fabric complements the warm wood tones in the arms of the chair. The smaller print on the contrast cord emphasizes the curved areas, further accenting the linear arms.

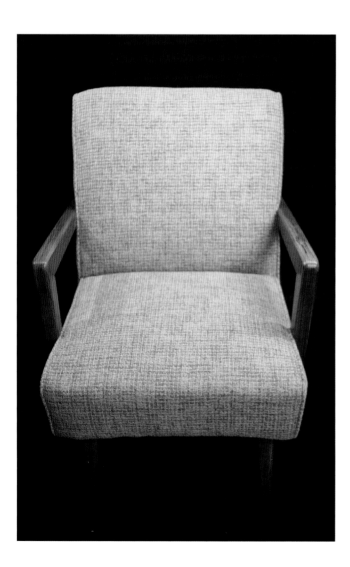

WHAT YOU NEED TO KNOW

Open arm chair slipcovers require careful planning. Consider how you will put on and take off the slipcover. Determine where to cut the fabric to fit the slipcover through and around the arms. To accommodate the arms, the slipcover will have more open edges, so you need to plan how you will secure the open edges to the chair. Options include Velcro, buttons, ties, or a combination of these, which requires planning prior to cutting the fabric.

For this slipcover, the sides of the seat are made in two welting-edged panels that fit on either side of the arm posts. The side back panels below the arms secure to the side seat panels with Velcro. The bottom of the slipcover is secured directly to the bottom of the chair to allow for the rocking motion of the chair.

It isn't possible to match a large print at the seams, but it is important to center the design on the IB, seat, and OB and to keep the design running uninterrupted down the inside back to the seat. Keep the cross grain of all the fabric pieces parallel to the floor or to the bottom of the chair.

In the directions that follow, the decorator fabric is fitted directly onto the chair, and no muslin pattern is made. If you don't feel confident using this method, make a muslin pattern first or make a trial slipcover from inexpensive fabric.

Anchoring

1. Measure and pin-mark center inside back (IB) and outside back (OB).

2. Leaving the roll of fabric on the floor behind the chair, pull the fabric up and over the back, centering the design by feeling for the pin marks under the fabric. Smooth the fabric down the IB. Cut the fabric at the seat, leaving about 6" (15 cm) for tuck-in allowance. Cut the sides of the IB, leaving about 6" (15 cm) beyond the upholstery seams. Anchor fabric on the IB with T-pins.

3. Pull fabric from the front of the chair up over the seat, centering the design. Fold under the top edge and align the design motif to the same motif on the IB about a hand's width above the seat. Smooth the fabric down over the seat, keeping the design centered. This will ensure the design continues uninterrupted. Cut the fabric several inches below the bottom of the chair. Anchor the fabric to the seat with a few T-pins.

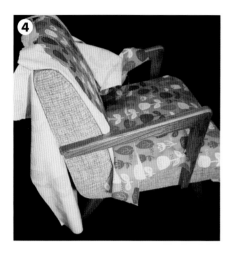

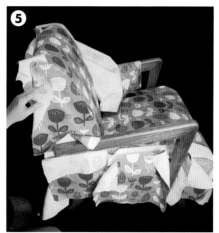

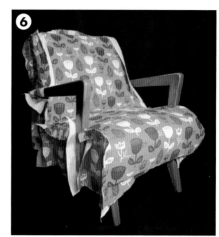

4. To cut a piece for the outside back (OB), find the center pattern at the top of the IB and line up a similar motif, making sure the pattern is going in an upward direction. Leave excess fabric along all the edges. Anchor the fabric to the OB with a few T-pins.

5. For the sides of the chair, you will need to cut separate pieces for each section. For this chair, each side has four pieces: side back above the arm, side back below the arm, side seat behind the vertical arm post, and side seat in front of the arm post. For each piece, center the design, and arrange the pieces so the design appears to run continuously from one piece to the next. Keep the cross grain parallel to the bottom of the chair for the side seat pieces. Run the lengthwise grain parallel to the chair back on the side back pieces. Leave ample excess fabric as you cut each piece. Anchor the pieces to the chair.

6. Now all pieces are rough-cut and ready for pin-fitting.

Pin-fitting

1. Determine the seam placement for the OB and IB where the curve at the top IB adjoins the OB at a right angle. This isn't necessarily how the upholsterer joined the pieces together.

2. Pin the IB to the OB at the center of the determined seam line; smooth the fabric, working from the center outward, pinning as you go.

3. Leaving a hand's width for tuck-in allowance, pin the IB to the seat. Near the sides, taper the allowance, and fit the slipcover snugly at the outer edges. Clip the seam allowances if necessary to allow the fabric to shape to the curved seat and back.

(continued)

4. Smooth seat fabric to wrap around front to seat underside; pin tucks in place at corners.

5. On the seat where the arm attaches to the chair, place pins at each side of the arm, and use an invisible marking pen to draw a line between the pins for placement of welting. Cut perpendicular to the line, stopping about 1" (2.5 cm) from the line. Then cut diagonally almost to the ends of the lines, allowing the fabric to fit around the arm. (This is called a Y-cut.) Repeat on the opposite side.

6. Pin-fit seat fabric and sides of seat together as tightly as possible. Clip as necessary to ease curves. On front side piece, mark the placement line for welting along the front of the arm post. On back side piece, mark the placement line for welting along the back of the arm post. Trim away excess fabric.

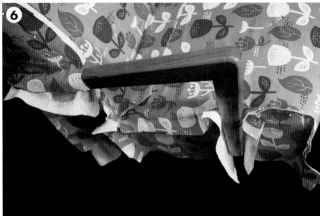

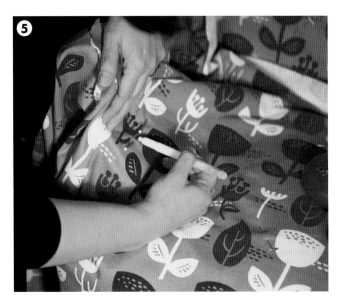

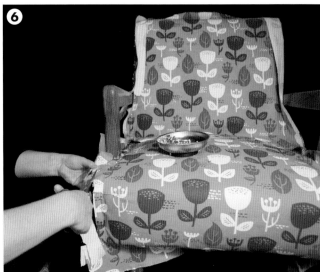

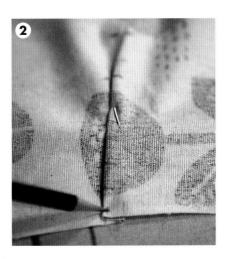

7. On the IB, place pins at top and bottom of arm, and use an invisible marking pen to draw a line between the pins for placement of welting. Y-cut to allow the fabric to fit around the arm. Repeat on the opposite side.

8. Pin-fit upper side back to IB and OB. Where the side panel meets the top of the arm, mark a line for placement of the welting. Pin-fit lower side back to IB, OB, and back seat panel. Where the side panel meets the bottom of the arm, mark a line for the closer hem.

9. Wrap the lower edges to the underside of the chair and mark all around at the inside edge of the chair frame.

10. Label each piece with blue painter's tape before removing the pin-fitted slipcover from the chair.

Preparing the Pieces

1. Mark the seam lines on the wrong side of the fabric, and trim the seam allowances to ½" (1.3 cm). Trim closure edges on side back seat and lower side backs to ¾" (2 cm). Allow 1" (2.5 cm) for hem on upper edge of side back flaps. Make notches and clip marks as necessary. Mark intersecting lines to help in matching seams. Remove pins from seams.

2. Mark tucks in front seat corners before removing pins.

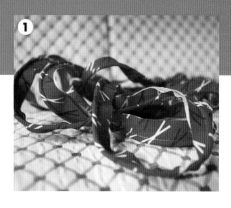

4. Pin IB to seat with tuck-in allowance; stitch.

5. Sew welting to the side seat panel edges that will be next to the chair arms. Sew the side seat panels to the seat.

6. Sew continuous welting from lower edge of back side seat, along edge of IB to lower edge of OB. Repeat on opposite side of slipcover.

7. Sew welting to lower edges of both upper back panels. Pin upper back side panels to inside back and outside back; stitch.

8. Turn under 1" (2.5 cm) hem at top of bottom back side panels and blind stitch or fuse in place. Stitch Velcro loop tape to the closure edges of the bottom back side panels. Stitch the bottom back side panels to the OB. Sew Velcro hook tape to the closure edge of the IB. (See chair photograph.)

9. Sew Velcro loop tape to the lower edges of the slipcover. Staple Velcro hook tape to the bottom of the chair.

10. If the arms on your chair do not go all the way to the back of the side, add small flaps of fabric to conceal the gap. See the difference in these two photos.

Sewing the Slipcover

1. Measure the edges to be welted. Cut bias strips for contrasting fabric (page 186) and make welting (page 184).

2. Serge/finish all raw edges. Fold the tucks of the front seat corners. Baste across the ends. Sew welting to both sides of the seat.

3. Sew welting to IB top seam. Pin the IB to the OB at the top; stitch the seam.

Putting on the Cover

1. Start from the top of the inside back, and shimmy the cover downward.

2. Smooth fabric out as the cover is put on; bring cover over the front of seat, and flip side flaps in place.

3. Push the seams to one side as the slipcover is put in place. In general, turn seams inward and downward, however, the direction of the seam can affect the fit and look of the welting or part of the cover. For example, if you didn't stitch close enough on one side of the welting, pushing the seam to the opposite side may push the cord over enough to "fill in" the space.

4. At the back of the seat, after smoothing the IB in place, start from center and move outward, pushing the tuck-in into place. Sometimes pushing down the seat with one hand while tucking will make it easier.

5. Overlap the bottom back flaps onto the Velcro edge of the IB to secure.

6. Secure the Velcro at the lower edges.

7. Use a steam iron or steamer to help mold the fabric to the chair.

Wing Chairs

The wing chair, a mainstay in many traditional living rooms, is often the preferred chair in the room. With its high back and extended sides, the wing chair can be very cozy and comfortable. So when it's time to change the room's décor, a slipcover updates the look and allows you to keep your favorite chair.

YOU WILL NEED

- muslin for making patterns
- decorator fabric
- contrasting fabric for welting (optional)
- cording for welting
- interfacing
- zipper, about 8" (20.5 cm) longer than back edge of cushion
- upholstery batting, if necessary, to pad the existing furniture
- polyurethane foam, 2" (5 cm) strips to insert at the sides and back of deck
- T-pins, tacks, or heavy-duty stapler and staples, for securing tacking strip to furniture
- button kit and six or seven forms for covered buttons, or six or seven decorator buttons

WHAT YOU NEED TO KNOW

The basic instructions for slipcovering a wing chair are the same as for the club chair slipcover shown on page 52, with a few modifications for the wings of the chair. This slipcover is designed with a center back button and buttonhole closure. If you prefer a zipper, simply follow the directions for the fitted slipcover on page 54.

Many wing chairs have exposed legs that are decorative, and you may wish to leave them exposed. If the legs are decorative or protrude away from the chair, making a long skirt unsuitable, make a short, self-lined gathered or box-pleated skirt.

Pin-fitting a Slipcover for a Wing Chair

1. Pin-fit the pattern for the inside and outside back as on page 54, steps 1 and 2; in step 1, mark a line 2" (5 cm) to the right and left corner, for overlap and underlap at the back center opening, and, in step 2, cut muslin 8" (20 cm) wider, not 15" (38 cm). Mark a line for the upper edge of the skirt.

2. Measure the length of the inside wing from the seam line at the top to the seam line at the top of the arm, and measure the width of the inside wing from the inside back across the wing at the widest point around the front to the seam line; add to this measurement the distance from the inside back to the outside back, measured across the top of the chair at the inside wing. Cut muslin about 6" (15 cm) wider and 4" (10 cm) longer than measurements. Mark the lengthwise grain line on the inside wing piece perpendicular to the floor.

3. Measure the length of the outside wing from the seam line at the top to the seam line along the arm, and measure the width of the wings across the widest point. Cut muslin about 4" (10 cm) wider and longer than measurements. Mark the lengthwise grain line on the outside wing piece.

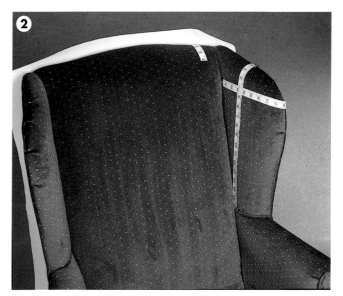

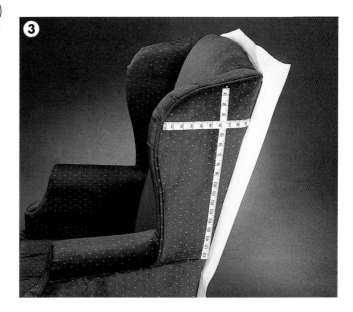

4. Pin the inside back piece to the chair. Follow step 4 on page 55, omitting reference to clipping along the arms and sides. Continue to mark a line on the inside back piece at the top of the chair along seam line of the inside back and wing, and clip to marked line at the point where the top of the chair meets the inside back.

5. Pin the outside wing piece in place, with grain line perpendicular to the floor and with the lower edge extending ½" (1.3 cm) beyond the seam line aligning with the arm. Smooth fabric upward; pin the outside wing to the outside back; mark seam.

6. Pin the inside wing in place, with the grain line perpendicular to the floor and with the lower edge extending ½" (1.3 cm) beyond the seam line along the arm. Push the fabric into the crevice at inside back; mark seam line and clip as in step 4. Pin the inside back to the outside back. Pin the inside wing to the outside wing at front; clip and trim the fabric at lower edge as necessary for a smooth fit. Pleat out excess fabric around curve of the inside wing piece, duplicating pleats in existing fabric. Mark fold lines of the pleats. Mark all seam lines on the pinned edges.

7. Follow steps 1 through 6 on pages 55 to 57 for a chair with a pleated arm; in step 4, make tucks if necessary at back of the arm where the arm meets the wing. Or follow steps 1 through 4 on pages 57 and 58, for an arm with a front section.

8. Follow page 58, steps 1 through 4, to pin-fit pattern for the deck. Pin-fit the skirt as on page 59, step 1; add 5" (12.8 cm) to each end of the skirt to allow for overlap, underlap, facings, and seam allowance at the center back closure and omit reference to seam at back corner for zipper. Follow page 58, step 2; if chair does not have a skirt, pin the skirt slipcover piece to the chair at marked upper skirt line, pinning ½" (1.3 cm) from upper raw edge of the skirt.

(continued)

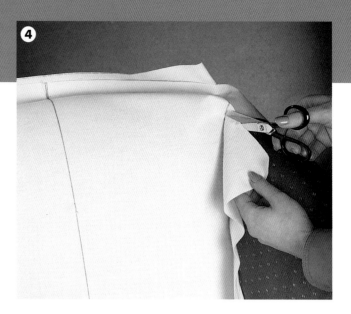

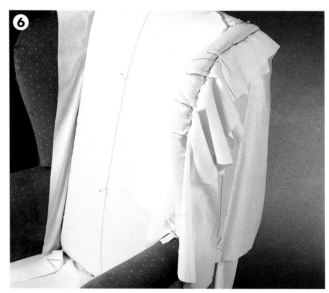

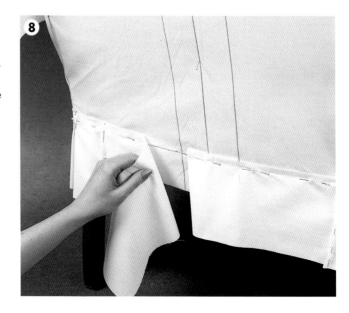

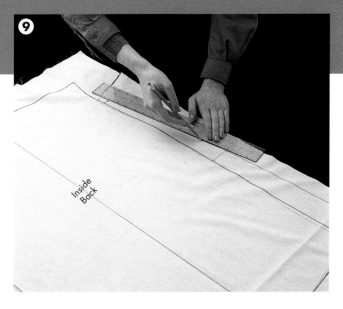

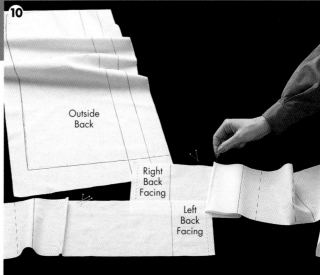

9. Follow page 000, step 1. Remove the muslin. True marked lines on the sides of the inside back piece. Insert a ruler into crevice at the top of the chair at the side of the inside back; record measurement for tuck-in. Repeat at the center and bottom along the side of the inside back. On sides of the inside back piece, mark points a distance from the marked line equal to tuck-in measurement at the top, center, and bottom. Draw a line connecting points. Mark points along the inside wing and inside arm pieces, corresponding to tuck-in points marked on the inside back. Draw a line connecting these points.

10. On the outside back, cut on the marked line 2" (5 cm) to the right of the center line; discard remaining portion of the outside back piece. Follow page 000, steps 3 through 6; in step 3, mark ½" (1.3 cm) seam allowances at the ends, and mark fold lines 3½" (9 cm) from the ends for center back facings. Continue as on page 000, steps 8 and 9.

Sewing a Slipcover for a Wing Chair with a Pleated Arm

1. Lay out and cut fabric for the slipcover as indicated on pages 86 to 88, using the outside back pattern to cut a right and left back piece. Cut two facing strips, 4" (10 cm) wide, for the center back with the length equal to measurement of the line at the center back. Align the long edges of the facing strips with the long edges of the outside back and trim the upper edge of facing strips to match the outer back piece.

2. Apply welting to upper and front edges of the outside arm, if desired, pivoting at the corner. Follow pages 62 and 63, steps 2 and 3. Pin the pleats in place around the inside wing. Check the fit over the wing of the chair. Baste in place on the seam line.

3. Staystitch a scant ½" (1.3 cm) from raw edges on the inside arm piece around the curve at the top of the arm; clip to stitching. Apply welting to the seam, if desired. Pin the lower edge of the inside wing to the top of the inside arm, right sides together; stitch from the inside back to ½" (1.3 cm) from the remaining side. Clip seam allowances.

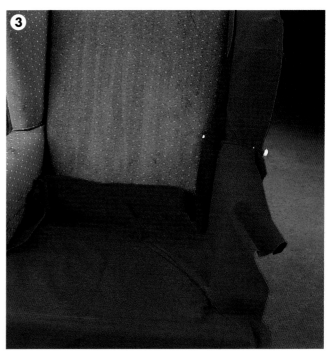

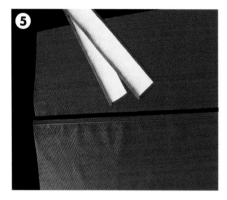

4. Stitch welting to the outside wing piece around the upper and front edges, if desired. Pin the inside wing and arm piece to the outside wing, right sides together; stitch around the upper and front edges from the seam line at the back to lower raw edge at the front.

5. Follow page 63, steps 4 to 6; in step 6, you will be pinning the inside wings and the inside arms to the inside back on both sides. Apply interfacing to the back facing pieces, within the seam allowances. Press under ½" (1.3 cm) along one long edge of the facing pieces. Apply welting to the left outside back piece, if desired.

6. Stitch the facing pieces to the outside back pieces, right sides together, using ½" (1.3 cm) seam allowances; press. Pin the facing to the outside back piece, wrong sides together; edgestitch close to the fold. Repeat for the other piece. Lap the left outside back piece over the right outside back piece; baste across the upper edges. Continue as indicated on page 64, step 7, omitting reference to leaving the seam open for the zipper.

7. Stitch the skirt pieces together; press the seams open. For a self-lined skirt, fold the skirt in half, right sides together. Stitch ½" (1.3 cm) from the raw edges at the ends; clip the corners. Turn the skirt right side out; align the upper edges, and press. Turn under 3" (7.5 cm) on each end of the skirt for facing; press.

8. Follow page 64, steps 9 and 10; in step 10, omit reference to the zipper. Mark placement of buttonholes on the left outside back piece, spacing evenly. Stitch the buttonholes. Stitch buttons to the right outside back piece at locations corresponding to the buttonholes. Continue as on page 64, steps 11 and 12.

Sewing a Slipcover for a Wing Chair with a Front Arm Piece

1. Follow step 1, opposite, for cutting and laying out the slipcover. Pin the pleats in place around the inside wing. Check fit over wing of the chair. Baste in place on the seam line. Follow steps 3 and 4. Apply welting to the upper edge of the outside arm piece. Stitch a horizontal seam, joining the outside arm to the inside arm. Pin and baste tucks at the front edge of the inside/outside arm. Apply welting to the front edge of the inside/outside arm.

2. Follow page 65, steps 2 and 3. Complete the vertical seam at the front edge of the outside arm. Follow page 63, step 6; you will be pinning the inside wings and the inside arms to the inside back on both sides. Apply interfacing to the back facing pieces, within seam allowances. Press up ½" (1.3 cm) along one long edge of the facing pieces. Apply welting to the left outside back piece, if desired. Complete the slipcover, following steps 6 through 8, opposite and above.

Cushion Covers

You can make slipcovers for cushions on benches or window seats, as well as for those on sofas or chairs. Most cushions fall into one of the three styles shown at left: knife-edge (top), waterfall (middle), and boxed (bottom). Any of these styles can be fitted flush to the front of the chair or T-shaped, wrapping around the front of the chair arms.

WHAT YOU NEED TO KNOW

To make it easier to insert the cushion, install a zipper across the back of the slipcover, extending about 4" (10 cm) onto each side. For cushions that are exposed on three sides, install a zipper across the back of the slipcover only. Use upholstery zippers, which are available in longer lengths than dressmaker zippers. For boxed and waterfall cushions, the tab of the zipper will be concealed in a pocket at the end of the zipper opening. This is an upholsterer's technique that gives a professional finish.

Boxed and knife-edge cushions can be sewn with or without welting at the seams. See page 184 for instructions on making and attaching welting. Knife-edge cushions on chairs or sofas usually have a welted seam around the center on sides where the cushion is exposed. If there are hidden sides, such as for a knife-edge seat cushion on a wing chair, the hidden sides are often constructed with a boxing strip. Waterfall cushions, more common in contemporary furniture, are sewn with one continuous piece of fabric wrapping over the front, from top to bottom. This style has a boxing strip around the sides and back and is usually made without welting.

Slipcovers for cushions can often be put on right over the existing upholstery fabric like the rest of the slipcover. There are circumstances, however, when it is better to remove the old cover and insert the cushion into the new slipcover. This is a better option if the slipcover fabric is lighter weight than the upholstery or if there is existing welting that will show through or cause wear on the new slipcover. For the best fit, pin-fit muslin to the existing cushion to make a pattern for the new cushion cover.

YOU WILL NEED

- muslin for making patterns
- decorator fabric
- zipper, about 8" (20.5 cm) longer than back edge of cushion
- fabric and cording for fabric-covered welting; or brush fringe or twisted welting
- high-density polyurethane foam, for making new cushion inserts
- electric knife (optional)
- polyester upholstery batting, for making new cushion inserts
- foam adhesive or hand needle and heavy thread, for making new cushion inserts
- large plastic bag or sheet of plastic
- vacuum cleaner with hose

Cutting Directions

Knife-edge Cushion

- If the cushion is rectangular, fairly flat, and soft like a pillow, cut a cushion cover top to the same dimensions as the original cushion plus 1" (2.5 cm) for seam allowances. Cut the cushion cover bottom 1" (2.5 cm) longer than the top to allow for ½" (1.3 cm) seam allowances at the zipper closure.

- To cover a rectangular cushion that has a thick, firm, foam insert, cut a top and bottom with the width and length equal to the cushion width and length plus the foam depth plus 1" (2.5 cm) for seam allowances.

- If continuous zipper tape is used, cut the zipper tape with the length equal to at least three-fourths of the cushion width, or purchase a conventional zipper with this approximate length.

- Cut fabric strips for the welting long enough to fit the welted section of the cushion.

Boxed Cushion

- Cut the top and bottom pieces 1" (2.5 cm) larger than the cushion size to allow for seam allowances. For boxed T-cushions, pin-fit a muslin pattern to ensure accurate cutting.

- Measure the original boxing strip between seams and add 1" (2.5 cm) for seam allowances. Cut the boxing strip with the length equal to the total measurement of the front and sides of the cushion. Excess length will be cut off during construction. If piecing is necessary, allow 1" (2.5 cm) for each seam, planning the placement of the seams out of view along the sides of the cushion.

- If continuous zipper tape is used, cut the zipper tape 8" (20.5 cm) longer than the back cushion measurement, or purchase an upholstery zipper of this approximate length. Cut two fabric strips for the zipper closure with the length equal to the length of the zipper tape and the width equal to half the cut width of the boxing strip plus ¾" (2 cm).

- If the cushion will be welted, cut fabric strips for the welting (page 186) with the length equal to twice the circumference of the cushion plus additional length for seaming strips, joining ends, and inconspicuously positioning seams.

Waterfall Cushion

- Pin-fit a muslin pattern for the continuous top/bottom piece. Cut a cushion top and bottom piece, using the pattern. Mark the end of the piece that will become the cushion top (with a directional print or napped fabric, the fabric will run in the correct direction only on the top).

- Cut the side boxing strips. Measure the original boxing strip between the seams and add 1" (2.5 cm) for seam allowances. Cut each boxing strip with the length equal to the side measurement of the cushion plus 1" (2.5 cm). Excess length will be cut off during construction.

- If continuous zipper tape is used, cut the zipper tape with the length equal to the back cushion measurement plus 8" (20.5 cm), or purchase an upholstery zipper of this approximate length. Cut two fabric strips for the zipper closure, with the length equal to the length of the zipper tape and the width equal to half the cut width of the boxing strip plus ¾" (2 cm).

Sewing a Knife-edge Cushion Cover

1. Fold in the lower edge of the cushion back 1¾" (4.5 cm), right sides together; press. Place the zipper alongside the fold and mark the fold at the location of the zipper stops. Stitch ½" (1.3 cm) from the fold, from the side to the first mark; backstitch. Machine-baste to the second mark; backstitch, then finish the seam to the opposite edge.

2. Cut on the fold. Press the seam allowances open.

3. Center the closed zipper facedown over the seam, with the stops at the marks. Glue-baste or pin the zipper tape to the seam allowances only. Finish the seam allowances, catching the zipper tape in the stitches.

4. Spread the cushion cover back flat, right-side up. Mark the top and bottom of the zipper coil with pins. Center a strip of ½" (1.3 cm) transparent tape over the seam from pin to pin. Topstitch a narrow rectangle along the edges of the tape, using a zipper foot. Stitch slowly as you cross the zipper just beyond the stops. Remove the tape. Pull threads to the underside and knot. Remove the basting stitches.

5. Make welting as on page 184. Sew the welting around the outer edge of the cushion cover top, following the continuous circle method.

6. Open the zipper partially. Pin the cover top and bottom with right sides together. With the wrong side of the top facing up, stitch just inside the first welting stitches, crowding the cording.

7. Turn the cover right-side out through the zipper opening.

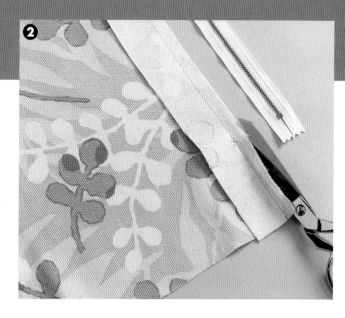

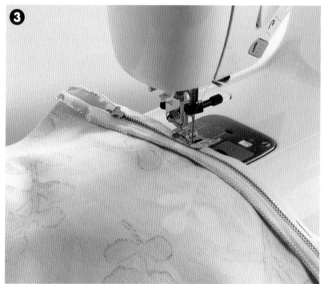

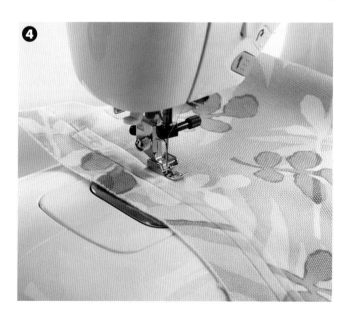

Sewing a Rectangular Boxed Cushion Cover

1. Make welting as on page 184. Sew the welting around the outer edge of the cushion top and cushion bottom, following the continuous circle method.

2. Press under ¾" (2 cm) seam allowance on one long edge of the zipper strip. Position the folded edge of the strip along the center of the zipper teeth, right-side up. Using a zipper foot, topstitch ⅜" (1 cm) from the fold. Repeat for the opposite side, making sure folds meet at the center of the zipper. If using continuous zipper tape, attach the zipper pull to the tape.

3. Center the zipper strip over the back edge of the cushion top, right sides together. Stitch the zipper strip to the cushion top, beginning and ending on the sides about 1½" (3.8 cm) beyond the corners. Clip into the zipper strip seam allowance at each corner to allow the fabric to spread, and pivot.

4. Align the center of the boxing strip to the front center of the cushion top, matching the print, if necessary; pin-mark the pieces separately. Smooth the boxing strip to the right front corner; mark with a ⅜" (1 cm) clip into the seam allowance. Smooth the boxing strip along the right side of the cushion top; pin the boxing strip to the cushion top about 6" (15 cm) from the back corner.

5. Stitch the boxing strip to the cushion top, beginning at the side pin and sewing a ½" (1.3 cm) seam. For a welted cover, use a welting foot or zipper foot. Match the clip mark to the front corner; pivot the stitching at the corner.

6. Continue stitching the boxing strip to the cushion top, matching the center marks. Clip once into the boxing strip seam allowance at the left front corner; pivot. Stop stitching about 6" (15 cm) from the back left corner.

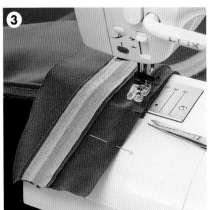

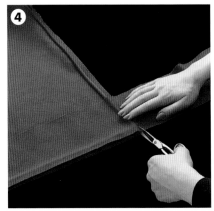

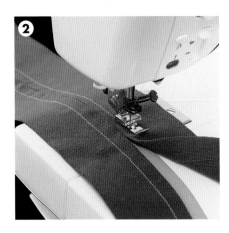

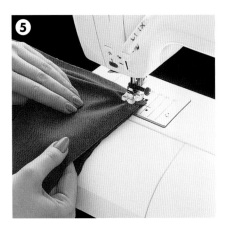

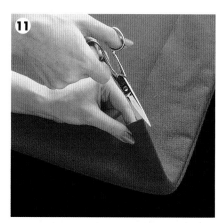

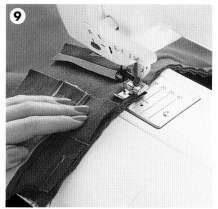

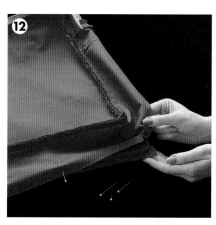

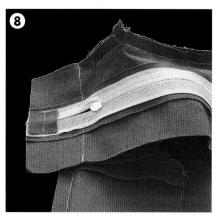

7. Cut the boxing strip 4" (10 cm) beyond the point where it overlaps the zipper pull end of the zipper strip. Pin the end of the boxing strip to the end of the zipper strip, right sides together, matching all cut edges.

8. Stitch together 2" (5 cm) from the end; pivot at the zipper tape. Stitch along the outer edge of the zipper tape to within ½" (1.3 cm) of the end; pivot. Place a small scrap of fabric over the zipper teeth. Stitch slowly across the teeth to the opposite side of the zipper tape, taking care not to break the needle; pivot. Stitch along the opposite side of the zipper tape until 2" (5 cm) from the end; pivot, and stitch to the edge.

9. Finger-press the seam allowance toward the boxing strip. Finish sewing the zipper strip and boxing strip to the cushion top. A small pocket forms to hide the zipper pull when the cover is closed.

10. Cut the opposite end of the boxing strip 1" (2.5 cm) beyond the point where it overlaps the end of the zipper strip. Pin the ends together. Stitch ½" (1.3 cm) from the ends, placing a scrap of fabric over the zipper teeth and stitching slowly. Turn the seam allowance toward the boxing strip. Finish sewing the zipper strip and boxing strip to the cushion top.

11. Fold the boxing strip straight across at the corner; mark the opposite side of the boxing strip with a ⅜" (1 cm) clip into the seam allowance. Repeat for all the corners.

12. Open the zipper partially. Pin the boxing strip to the cushion bottom, matching the clip marks to the corners. Stitch. Turn the cover right-side out through the zipper opening.

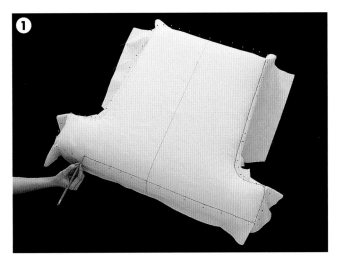

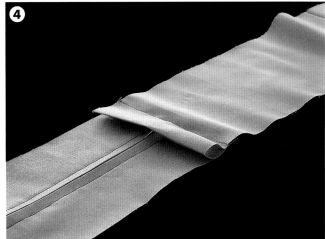

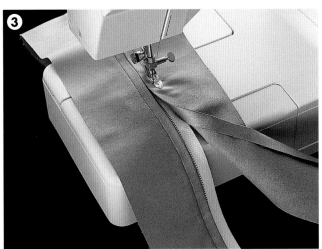

Sewing a Boxed T-cushion Cover

1. Cut muslin about 4" (10 cm) larger than the top of the cushion; mark the grain line at the center of the fabric. Place the muslin over the cushion; pin along the seam line, smoothing out the fabric. Mark the seam line along the pin marks.

2. Remove the muslin. True the seam lines, using a straightedge. Fold the muslin in half to check that the piece is symmetrical; make any necessary adjustments. Add ½" (1.3 cm) seam allowances to the pattern. Cut the pieces as in the cutting directions on page 92.

3. Press under a ½" (1.3 cm) seam allowance on one long edge of each zipper strip. Position the folded edges of the strips along the center of the zipper teeth, right sides up. Using a zipper foot, topstitch ⅜" (1 cm) from folds.

4. Press under 2" (5 cm) on one short end of the boxing strip. Lap the boxing strip over the zipper strip to cover the zipper tab. Stitch through all layers 1½" (3.8 cm) from the folded edge of the boxing strip.

5. Make and apply welting as on page 184. Stitch welting to the right side of top and bottom pieces.

6. Place the boxing strip on the slipcover top, right sides together; center the zipper on the back edge. Start stitching 2" (5 cm) from the zipper end, crowding the cording. Clip the corners as you come to them; stop stitching 4" (10 cm) from the starting point.

7. Clip to mark the seam allowances at the ends of the boxing strip. Stitch the boxing strip ends together. Trim off excess fabric; finger-press the seam open. Finish stitching the boxing strip to the slipcover top.

8. Fold the boxing strip, and clip the seam allowance to mark the lower corners; be sure all corners are aligned with the corners on the slipcover top. Open the zipper.

9. Place the boxing strip and slipcover bottom right sides together. Match the clips of the boxing strip to the corners of the slipcover bottom; stitch. Turn the cover right-side out.

10. Fold the cushion to insert it into the cover. Stretch the cover from front to back. Close the zipper. Smooth the cover from center to edges. Stretch the welting taut from corner to corner to square the cushion.

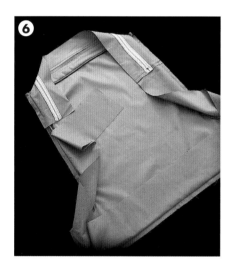

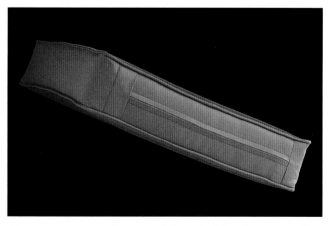

Alternative zipper placement (above). If the slipcover will be exposed on three sides, install the zipper across the back of the slipcover without extending it around the sides.

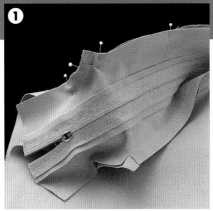

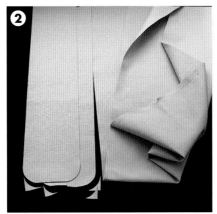

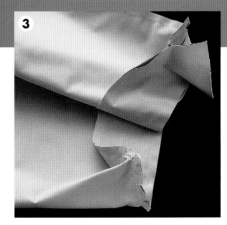

Matching Patterned Fabric

1. Cut the slipcover top and boxing strips so the pattern matches at the front seam lines. Notch the front corners on the upper and lower edges of the boxing strip.

2. Stitch the boxing strip to the front edge of the slipcover top first. Then continue stitching the boxing strip to the slipcover top and bottom.

Sewing a Waterfall Cushion Cover

1. Follow steps 2 and 3 for the boxed cushion on page 94. Fold the zipper strip straight across at the corner; mark the opposite edge with a ⅜" (1 cm) clip into the seam allowance. Repeat at the other corner. Pin the zipper strip to the back edge of the cushion bottom, matching the clip marks to the corners. Stitch, beginning and ending about 1½" (3.8 cm) beyond the corners.

2. Mark the center of the front short end of each side of the boxing strip; round the front corners of the side boxing strips slightly. Mark the outer edges of the top/bottom cushion at the center front. Staystitch a scant ½" (1.3 cm) from the outer edges of the top/bottom piece a distance on either side of the marks equal to the cushion height.

3. Clip the seam allowances to the staystitching every ½" (1.3 cm). Pin the side boxing strip to the top/bottom, right sides together, aligning the center marks. Check to see that corresponding points on the top/bottom match up directly across from each other on the boxing strip. Sew ½" (1.3 cm) seam, beginning and ending 6" (15 cm) from the back corners. Repeat on the opposite side.

4. Follow steps 7 through 10 on page 95. Open the zipper partially. Finish sewing the boxing strip to the top/bottom on both sides. Turn the cushion cover right-side out through the zipper opening.

Making a New Cushion Insert

1. Cut foam to the finished size and shape of the cushion, using an electric knife. Hold the knife blade perpendicular to the foam to ensure straight sides. Or take your measurements to the store and have the foam cut there.

2. Wrap polyester batting over the foam from front to back. Trim the sides and back so that the cut edges overlap about 1" (2.5 cm) at the center of the cushion.

3. Apply spray foam adhesive to the cut edges of the batting and the back of the cushion. Overlap the edges, and press them firmly together to seal. Or whipstitch the edges together, using a large needle and heavy thread. Repeat for the sides.

4. Trim excess batting vertically at the corners. Apply adhesive, and press the edges together to seal. Or whipstitch the corners in place.

5. Fold the cushion in half from front to back. Insert the cushion into the opening and gradually work it toward the front of the cover (or use the vacuum method at right). Stretch the cover to fit the cushion. Check to see that the cushion is inserted symmetrically, with equal fullness on both sides. Turn the seam allowances toward the boxing strip all around the cushion. Zip the cover closed, hiding the zipper pull in the pocket.

1. Insert the prepared cushion into a lightweight trash bag or wrap it with lightweight plastic. Overlap the open edge of the plastic at one end. Insert the vacuum hose into a small hole cut in the plastic or wrap the plastic around the hose and hold tightly.

2. Press the end of the hose against the cushion. Turn on the vacuum. Suck air from the cushion until it slips easily into the cover. Turn off the vacuum and remove the plastic, allowing air to reenter the cushion.

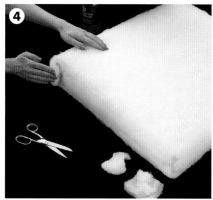

PILLOWS, BEAN BAG CHAIRS, AND TUFFETS

Like slipcovers, pillows can change the look of any room in an instant—for a minimal cost. They add color and pizzazz to a neutral background, subtly complement a print sofa or chair, or add a touch of fun and comfort to any surface. And best of all, you can make pillows in any shape or size to fit your needs. Whether they are tailored pillows to accent furniture or oversized pillows designed to serve as bean bag chairs, pillows are as much fun to make as they are to use.

Pillow Basics

When is a pillow more than just a pillow? When you use it as a palette to express your creativity! Beautiful fabrics await your pillow-making skills, but that isn't all. There are also gorgeous trims, edge finishes, and clever closure options you can incorporate to give your pillow a designer look.

Before you begin any pillow style, it is helpful to understand basic techniques and decide which ones apply to your project.

STUFFING OPTIONS

Premade pillow forms are available in a wide variety of shapes and sizes, and come filled with your choice of polyester fiberfill, feathers, or even bamboo. You can also make your own form using muslin and fill it with the stuffing of your choice.

CLOSURE OPTIONS

All pillows require some type of closure to allow for stuffing the pillow or adding an insert. The closure can be as simple and subtle as slipstitching an opening closed or creating an overlap, or it can be more decorative, making use of buttons or ties. The following options are suitable for flange pillows (see page 118) and box pillows (see page 122), as well as knife-edge pillows (page 116).

Zipper Closures

Conventional polyester zippers can be inserted in a seam between pieces of the pillow back. The seam can be centered in the pillow back or placed close to one edge so that it is less visible. Invisible zippers, which must be installed using a special presser foot, are usually placed in the seam between the pillow front and back, where they almost disappear.

Make the zipper closure long enough so that removing and inserting the pillow form will not strain the zipper ends. As a general rule, use a zipper that is at least three-fourths of the pillow width. Zippers can be shortened, if necessary.

How to Insert a Conventional Zipper

1. Cut the pillow back 1" (2.5 cm) wider than the front to allow for ½" (1.3 cm) seam allowances at the closure. To center the closure in the pillow back, fold the pillow back panel in half, right sides together.

2. Center the zipper on the folded edge. Mark the fold at the location of the zipper stops. Stitching ½" (1.3 cm) from the fold, begin at one edge and stitch to the mark, then backstitch. Stitch to the opposite mark using a basting stitch. At the mark, shorten the stitch length and stitch to the edge, then backstitch.

3. Cut along the fold and press the seam allowances open.

4. Center the closed zipper facedown over the seam, with the stops at the marks. Pin the tapes to the seam allowances or secure them in place with double-sided basting tape. Finish the seam allowances with zigzag stitches, catching the zipper tapes in the stitching.

5. Spread the pillow panel flat with the right side up. Mark the top and bottom of the zipper teeth with pins. Center a strip of transparent tape, measuring ½" (1.3 cm) wide, over the seam from pin to pin. Use a zipper foot and topstitch along the edges of the tape to create a rectangle.

6. Finish the pillow, following the general instructions for the pillow style. Rather than leaving an opening for turning, open the zipper before stitching the final seam. Turn right side out through the zipper opening, insert the pillow form, and close the zipper.

How to Shorten a Zipper

1. Close the zipper. Mark the desired length on the zipper tape. Drop or cover the sewing machine feed dogs and attach a button or appliqué presser foot. Set the machine to the widest zigzag setting, and stitch in place across the zipper teeth for several stitches at the mark.

2. Cut off the excess zipper ½" (1.3 cm) below the stitches.

How to Insert an Invisible Zipper

1. Open the zipper; press open the zipper tape from the wrong side to unroll the coils. Center the zipper along one long edge of the pillow back. Mark the right side of the pillow back at the ends of the zipper coil; transfer the marks to the pillow front. Use a removable fabric marker or chalk to mark the ½" (1.3 cm) seam line on the fabric.

2. Position the open zipper on the pillow back with right sides together, aligning the zipper coil with the seam line and the coil ends with the marks. Pin in place or secure with double-sided basting tape. Finish the seam allowance with zigzag stitches, catching the zipper tape in the stitching.

3. Attach an invisible zipper foot to the machine. Position the top of the zipper coil under the appropriate groove of the foot. Adjust the needle position so the stitching will be very close to the coil; on heavier fabrics, position the needle slightly away from the coil. Start stitching at the top of the zipper and continue until the foot touches the zipper pull at the bottom.

4. Secure the other side of the zipper to the pillow front, as in step 2. Position the coils under the zipper foot; slide the zipper foot on the adapter to the opposite side, and adjust the needle position. The bulk of the fabric will be on the opposite side of the needle. Stitch until the zipper foot touches the zipper pull.

5. Close the zipper; pin the pillow front and back right sides together above and below the zipper. Adjust the zipper foot, making sure it is as close as possible to the zipper. Stitch the rest of the seam.

6. Open the zipper. Attach the general purpose presser foot and finish the pillow, following the general instructions. Rather than leaving an opening for turning, simply open the zipper before stitching the final seam.

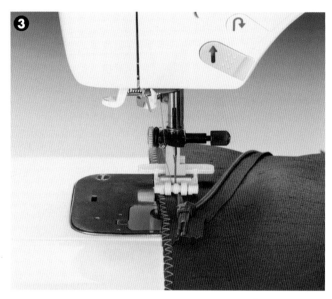

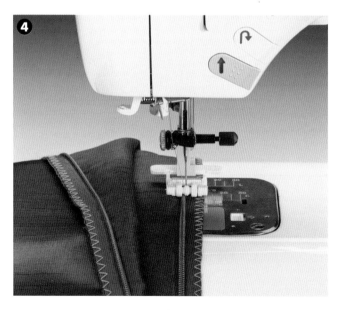

How to Sew an Overlapping Closure

A plain lapped closure where two hemmed edges overlap is one of the quickest and easiest closures to make. For small to medium pillow sizes, a 2" (5 cm) overlap is sufficient, but increase the overlap width up to 4" (10 cm) for large to extra-large pillows.

1. To make a closure with a standard 2" (5 cm) overlap, cut two rectangles for the pillow back with the length equal to the finished pillow height, plus 1" (2.5 cm) for seam allowances. The width of each rectangle should be equal to half the finished pillow width plus 3½" (8.8 cm).

2. On the edges that will overlap, press under a doubled 1" (2.5 cm) hem on each piece. Topstitch the hem in place close to the inner fold.

3. With right sides up, overlap the hemmed edges 2" (5 cm); the inner folds will align.

4. Baste across the hem ends.

5. Follow the general pillow instructions to finish the pillow. Turn the pillow right-side out through the overlapped hems and press.

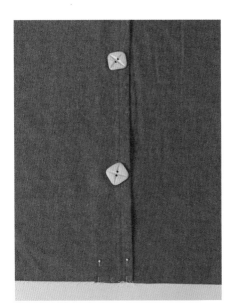

How to Sew a Hook-and-Loop-Tape Lapped Closure

1. Cut two rectangles for the pillow back with the length equal to the finished pillow length, plus 1" (2.5 cm) for seam allowances. The width of each pillow should be equal to half the finished pillow width plus 3" (7.5 cm).

2. On the edges that will overlap, press under a doubled 1" (2.5 cm) hem on each piece. On one piece only, topstitch the hem in place close to the inner fold.

3. Cut strips of hook-and-loop tape, ¾" (2 cm) wide, 3" (7.5 cm) shorter than the hemmed edge. Center the loop side of the tape on the right side of the stitched hem on one panel. Stitch around the outer edges of the tape.

4. On the remaining piece, unfold the pressed hem. Center the hook side of the tape on the right of the fabric between the two pressed folds. Stitch the edges of the tape in place. Refold the hem and topstitch in place close to the inner fold.

5. Overlap the edges with the top and bottom edges even, and seal the tape. Baste across the hem ends.

6. Follow the general instructions to finish the pillow. Open the closure and turn right-side out through the opening. Press the edges and seal the opening closed.

How to Sew a Buttoned Lapped Closure

1. Follow step 1 for the hook-and-loop closure, but stitch both hems in place.

2. Determine the buttonhole size based on the size of the buttons you will be using. Evenly space and mark the buttonhole placements on one hemmed edge, parallel to the edge. Stitch the buttonholes.

3. Overlap the hemmed edges with the buttonholes on top. Mark a button placement through the center of each buttonhole onto the under-lapped hem. Sew on the buttons.

4. Overlap and button the panels together. Baste across the hem ends.

5. Follow the general instructions to finish the pillow. Open the closure and turn right-side out through the opening. Press the edges and seal the opening closed.

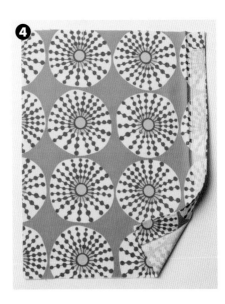

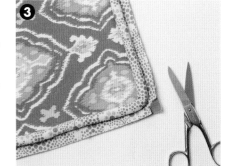

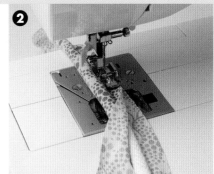

EDGE FINISHES

Fabric-covered welting and twisted cord define the pillow edges and give it a classic, tailored look. Other trims are available in a range of styles. Ruffles, or pleats can be made with matching or contrasting fabric. In addition to being suitable for knife-edge pillows, the following edge finishes can be applied to box pillows.

Welting

Welting is made by covering cotton cording with bias-cut fabric strips. Select the cording size that is most proportionate to the size of the pillow and compatible with the weight of the fabric.

How to Make Fabric-Covered Welting

1. To cut bias strips, fold the fabric diagonally, aligning the cut end to the selvage. Cut strips parallel to the fold, 1" (2.5 cm) wider than the cording circumference. Piece strips together to a length a few Inches (cm) longer than the distance to be welted.

2. Fold the fabric strip around the cording, right-side out, aligning the raw edges. Using a cording foot or zipper foot, machine-baste close to the cording. Keep the cording straight and smooth as you sew.

3. Starting 2" (5 cm) from the edge of the welting, stitch the welting to the right side of the pillow, aligning the raw edges. Clip and ease the welting at corners; ease the welting around curves.

4. Stop stitching 2" (5 cm) from the point where the ends will meet. Cut the cord even with the beginning cord end, but do not cut the bias strip. Cut off the excess bias strip so it overlaps the other end by 2" (5 cm).

5. Fold under 1" (2.5 cm) on the overlapping bias strip and wrap it around the beginning of the welting. Finish stitching the welting to the panel edge.

6. Finish the pillow, following the general instructions for the style. On seams that carry welting, use a cording foot or zipper foot. With the wrong side of the welted piece facing up, stitch inside the previous stitching line, stitching as close as possible to the welting.

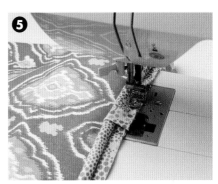

Twisted Cord

Twisted cord is made with fiber-covered cords that are twisted together and sewn to a "lip" that is inserted in the seam. It is available in several widths and in a wide range of colors, styles, and fibers. For easier stitching and to prevent the lip from showing on the outside of the pillow, it is applied to the pillow back first and the ends of the welting are twisted together to join them inconspicuously.

Twisted cord tends to unravel easily. Before cutting trim to a workable length, wrap a piece of tape around the cord and then cut through the center of the tape. Before making final cuts, saturate the trim with liquid fray preventer or fabric glue and allow it to dry completely, then cut through the center of the sealed area.

How to Attach Twisted Cord

1. If you haven't already done so, taper the corners of square or rectangular pillow panels as instructed on page 116.

2. Begin at the center of one edge and pin the twisted cord to the back pillow panel with right sides up, allowing for 3" (7.5 cm) to overlap on each end. Align the edge of the lip with the edge of the pillow panel. Mark each corner with a pin. Remove the trim.

3. Hand-tack the lip to the cord ¼" (6 mm) from each side of each corner pin. Clip the lip up to, but not into, the cording at each pin mark, then remove the pins. This allows the trim to turn the corners smoothly.

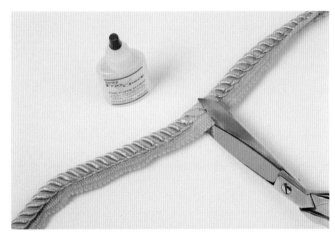

4. Use double-sided basting tape or pin the cord lip to the pillow panel as planned in step 2, aligning the clips with the corners. Beginning 3" (7.5 cm) from one end of the cording, use a zipper foot and stitch the cording to the pillow panel. Round the cord at the corner and stitch only on the fabric. Leave 1½" (3.8 cm) unstitched between the ends.

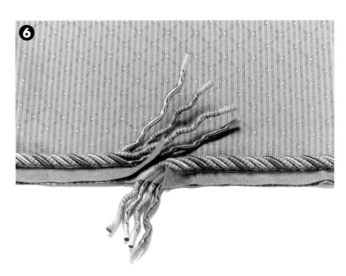

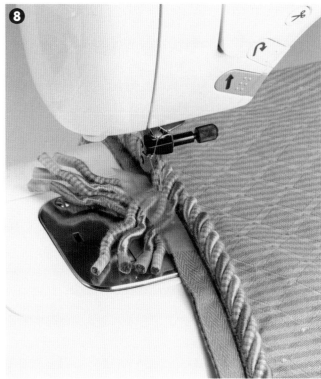

5. Loosen the cord from the lip in the area of the join. Trim the lip ends so they overlap 1" (2.5 cm). Separate the cord plies; wrap the end of each ply with tape. Arrange the plies so those on the right turn up and those on the left turn down.

6. Insert the plies on the right under the crossed lip ends, twisting and pulling them down until the cording is returned to its original shape. Secure in place with tape.

7. Twist and pull the plies on the left over the plies on the right until the twisted ends look like continuous twisted welting from both sides. Tape in place.

8. Position the zipper foot on the left of the needle, if possible. Place the pillow panel to the right of the needle; this will allow you to stitch in the direction of the cord twists, rather than against them. Machine-baste through all layers to secure the cording. If you are unable to adjust your machine to stitch in this position, remove the presser foot and stitch manually over the thick cords. Make sure the presser foot lever is down so the thread tension is engaged.

9. Finish the pillow, following the general instructions for the style. On seams that carry the twisted cord, use a zipper foot. With the wrong side of the welted piece facing up, stitch inside the previous stitching line, as close to the cording as possible.

Fringe

Fringes are available in a wide variety of fibers—both synthetic and natural—as well as in an abundance of styles and colors. Some fringes have decorative headings that are designed to be sewn onto the surface of the pillow, while others have plain, utilitarian headings that are intended to be sewn into a seam.

How to Attach Fringe with a Plain Heading

1. If you haven't already done so, taper the corners of square or rectangular pillow panels as instructed on page 116.

2. Begin at the center of one edge and pin the fringe header to the back pillow panel with right sides up, allowing for 1" (2.5 cm) to overlap on each end. Align the edge of the lip with the edge of the pillow panel. Mark each corner with a pin. Remove the trim.

3. Hand-tack the top of the lip to the fringe ¼" (6 mm) from each side of each corner pin. Clip the lip up to, but not into, the fringe lip at each pin mark, then remove the pins. This allows the trim to turn the corners smoothly.

4. Use double-sided basting tape or pin the fringe lip to the pillow panel as planned in step 2, aligning the clips with the corners. Beginning at one end of the fringe, use a regular foot and stitch the fringe lip to the pillow panel at the base of the lip. Round the cord at the corner and stitch only on the fabric. Stop stitching 1" (2.5 cm) from the beginning trim end.

5. Tape and cut the trim end to butt or slightly overlap the beginning end, depending on the weight of the trim. Continue stitching the trim in place.

6. Finish the pillow, following the general instructions for the style. On seams that carry the fringe, use a zipper foot. With the wrong side of the fringed piece facing up, stitch inside the previous stitching line, staying as close to the fringe as possible.

How to Attach Fringe with a Decorative Heading

1. Assemble the pillow but do not stuff it. Apply the fringe around the edges of the pillow front using one of the following techniques.

2. For lightweight trims, pin the trim heading around the edges, mitering the corners, and hand stitch in place. Tack the overlapping edges of the mitered corners together. For medium-or heavyweight trims, glue the trim in place using fabric adhesive, making sure to glue the edges of the mitered corners. Be careful not to use too much of the fabric adhesive; it can ooze around the edges and show after it is dry.

3. To end the trim, overlap the heading end by 1" (2.5 cm) and snip off the excess trim. Turn the heading under ½" (1.3 cm) and glue to the underlying heading.

4. For lighter weight trims, use fusible web tape and follow the manufacturer's instructions to fuse the fringe heading in place. For synthetic-fiber headings, use a press cloth to prevent the heat from melting the fibers.

Brush Fringe (1)

A dense row of yarns and/or other fibers that are cut to the same length, brush fringes are available with plain or decorative headings and may even be embellished with beads. The cut edge is usually secured with a chain stitch, which should not be removed until you have finished the pillow. This prevents the ends from accidentally getting caught in the seam as you stitch. After the pillow is finished, simply pull one end of the chain stitch and it will unravel. Fluff the fringe gently with your fingers or with steam.

Loop Fringe (2)

Loop fringe is also a dense row of yarns and/or other fibers, but the ends are looped rather than cut. The loops may be the same length or varied lengths, and the heading may be decorative or plain.

Tassel and Ball Fringes (3)

Made with a continuous row of tassels or pompoms, or a combination of both, tassel and ball fringes are available in a variety of fibers and colors, and some may also be embellished with beads. The heading may be decorative or plain.

Bullion Fringe (4)

A continuous row of twisted cords attached to a plain or decorative heading, bullion fringe ranges in style from very heavy, long fringe to lightweight, short fringe with single-color or multicolored cords. Cotton bullion fringe is generally casual while rayon or acetate fringe adds a more formal and elegant touch.

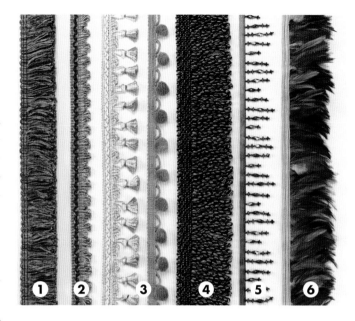

Beaded Fringe (5)

Beaded fringe is available in a vast array of colors, combinations, and styles, ranging from fun and funky to elegant. The fringe may consist entirely of beads strung side by side, in the same or varying lengths, or the beads may be combined with tassels, pom-poms, or other trims like sequins. Beaded fringe is available with either decorative or plain headings.

Feather Fringe (6)

Use this fringe to add a touch of fun to pillows that are meant to be more decorative than useful. They are available in a variety of feather types, lengths, and colors, ranging from natural to brightly dyed. Feather fringes usually have a plain heading.

Flat Trims

Flat trims are available in a variety of fibers, beads, sequins, feathers, or fur. They can be found in a range of colors and widths and are always intended as surface embellishments. Hand stitch them in place or use fabric adhesive. Use them to accent edges or seams, or to create free-form designs on the pillow surface. Flat trims are suitable for any pillow style.

How to Attach Flat Trims

1. To create a free-form design on the pillow surface, use a fabric marker or chalk and draw the design on the pillow panel to be embellished.

2. Center the trim over the marked lines and hand stitch or glue in place.

3. You can also combine flat trims with fringes for surface embellishment. Hand stitch or glue fringe with a plain heading in place. Glue or stitch flat trim over the heading.

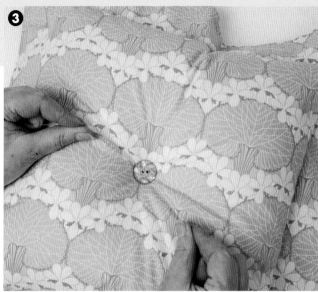

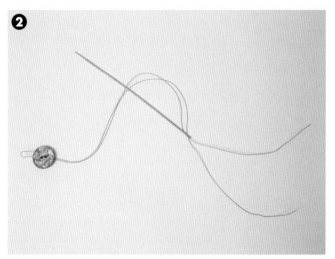

Tufting

Tufting adds interest and dimension to knife-edge pillows, as well as flange and box styles. You can add a single large button in the center of a pillow or add multiple tucks with smaller buttons. It's easy to do and all you need are two same-size buttons with shanks or large holes, waxed button thread, and a 6" (15 cm) upholstery needle or other long, large-eye needle.

How to Tuft a Pillow

1. On the finished pillow, mark the center of the top and bottom panels for a center tuft, or mark evenly-spaced placements for multiple tufts.

2. Cut a 12" (30.5 cm) length of waxed button thread. Center the shank of one button on the thread or slide the buttonholes onto the center of the thread. Insert both ends of the thread through the eye of the needle.

3. Stitch through the top of the pillow at the mark, bringing the needle out at the corresponding mark on the bottom.

4. Remove the needle and insert one thread through the remaining button shank or both thread ends through the buttonholes. Tie the thread ends together, pulling tightly to indent the surface. Knot the thread securely. Trim the thread ends at least ¼" (6 mm) from the knot.

Five Pillow Styles

Pillows can be made in several distinctive styles: knife-edge, flange, mock box, box, and bolster. Within each of these styles, you can design countless pillows in a wide range of fabrics, using decorative techniques and embellishments to suit every décor and budget.

Make pillows to fit ready-made square, rectangular, round, and bolster pillow forms. For pillows in nonstandard sizes and shapes, make forms to fit and fill them with the loose stuffing of your choice. For pillows without removable inserts, stuff the filling directly into the pillow cover.

YOU WILL NEED

- decorator fabric
- pillow form or polyester fiberfill
- zipper, hook-and-loop tape, or buttons for closure of choice (optional)
- optional embellishments, such as welting, twisted cord, or other trims

KNIFE-EDGE PILLOWS

The knife-edge pillow is the most basic of pillow styles. At its simplest it is two matching fabric panels sewn together around their perimeters and slipstitched closed after the pillow form is inserted. But it can be so much more! Think of this basic style as a blank canvas for creativity—you can piece the panels with contrasting fabrics, add welting, a ruffle, or trim to the edges, add interesting closures, or tuft the finished pillow.

These pillows can be square, rectangular, round, or shaped in a creative design, and stuffed with purchased pillow forms or with polyester fiberfill. Because the center of the pillow is thicker than the edges, square and rectangular knife-edge pillows tend to develop "dog ears" on the corners. You can stuff the corners lightly with fiberfill to minimize this look, or avoid it altogether with the corner tapering technique described in steps 2 to 4, as follows.

How to Make a Basic Knife-Edge Pillow

Note: Follow these instructions to make a basic pillow with an opening for stuffing that is slipstitched closed. To create a different type of closure, refer to Closure Options on page 102 before cutting.

1. Determine the desired finished size of your pillow and add 1" (2.5 cm) to both directions for seam allowances. Cut the pillow front and back panels along the fabric grain lines.

2. To taper the corners, fold the front panel into fourths. Mark a point halfway between the corner and the fold on each open side. At the corner, mark a point ½" (1.3 cm) from each edge. Draw a line connecting the points.

3. Cut along the marked lines, cutting through all four layers of fabric.

Cutting Heavy Fabric

If the fabric is heavy, mark and trim one corner, then use it as a pattern to trim the three remaining corners.

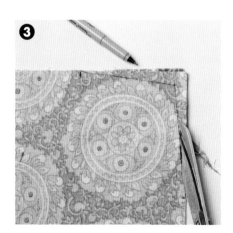

4. Unfold the front panel and use it as a pattern for trimming the back.

5. Pin the pillow front to the back, right sides together. Stitch the edges together, using a ½" (1.3 cm) seam allowance and pivoting at the corners. Leave an opening on one lengthwise-grain side for stuffing the pillow.

Opening Size

If you will be inserting a pillow form, leave an opening about two-thirds the length of the side. If you will be stuffing with fiberfill, leave an opening that is large enough for your hand to fit through.

6. Press the seams flat. Then turn back the upper seam allowance and press with the tip of the iron in the crease of the seam. Press both ½" (1.3 cm) seam allowances under along the opening.

7. Turn the pillow cover right-side out. Square up the corners, using a point turner, chopstick, or similar pointed utensil inserted through the opening. Press lightly.

8. Compress and insert the pillow form, making sure the form sits squarely inside the cover; add fiberfill in the corners, if necessary. Or stuff the pillow with fiberfill.

9a. Pin the opening closed, aligning the pressed folds. Edgestitch by machine.

9b. Pin the opening closed, aligning the pressed folds. Slipstitch the opening closed by hand.

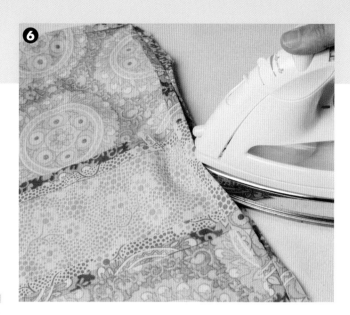

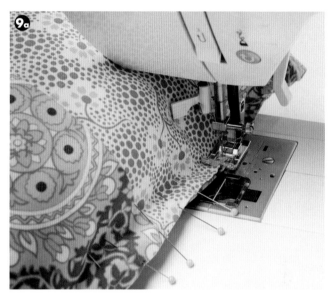

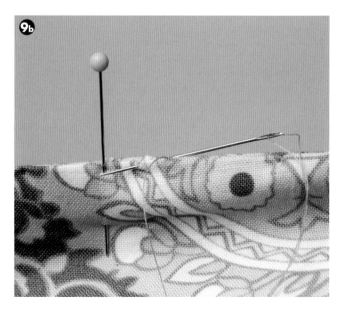

FLANGE PILLOWS

A flange pillow is essentially a knife-edge pillow with a flat fabric extension that goes beyond the stuffed portion of a pillow.

There are several ways to make a flange. A single flange is formed from two layers of fabric seamed together around the outer edge, then stitched wrong sides together along the inner edge. For a decorative touch, the flange portion of the front and back panels can be pieced with a contrasting fabric.

For a double flange pillow, two reversible panels are sewn together the desired distance from the edge to create a flange. Raw-edge flange pillows are made with two layers of fabrics that do not have a wrong side or ravel, such as felt, real or faux suede, or real or faux leather.

The width of a flange depends on the size of your pillow. It looks best to keep it proportionate—a width of 2" to 3" (5 cm to 7.5 cm) is attractive on medium-size pillows; larger pillows can have wider flanges. On lighter weight fabric or for wider flanges, apply fusible interfacing to the wrong side of the fabric to give the flange stability.

The easiest way to make a flange pillow is to stitch the opening closed by machine, but you can also use an overlapping or a zipper closure in the center of the back panel by piecing the back with two panels. Follow the overlapped closure instructions on page 105 to overlap two panels. Or for a zipper, follow the conventional zipper instructions on page 103 and apply the zipper only to the portion of the back that will be stuffed. Sew the fabric edges together at each end of the zipper to the edge of the panels.

How to Make a Single Flange Pillow

1. Determine the finished size of the stuffed area of the pillow plus twice the width of the flange. Add 1" (2.5 cm) to the width and length to allow for ½" (1.3 cm) seam allowances. Cut out the pillow front and back, aligning the sides to the fabric grain lines.

2. Follow steps 5 through 7 for the knife-edge pillow (page 117). Mark the depth of the flange from the seamed outer edge. Pin the layers together along the marked line to prevent them from shifting. Stitch on the marked line, leaving an opening of the same size parallel to the outer opening.

3. Insert the pillow form or stuff the inner area with polyester fiberfill; do not stuff the flange. Topstitch the inner edge of the flange closed, using a zipper foot.

4. Slipstitch the outer opening closed or edgestitch around the pillow.

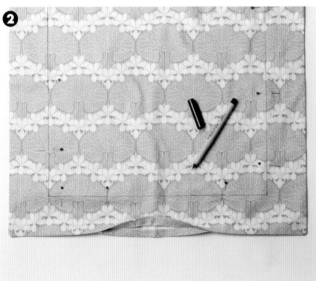

How to Make a Double Flange Pillow

1. Determine the finished size of the stuffed area of the pillow plus twice the width of the flange. Add 1" (2.5 cm) to the width and length to allow for ½" (1.3 cm) seam allowances. Cut out the pillow front and back, aligning the sides to the fabric grain lines. For a raw-edge double flange pillow, cut two panels. For a double flange pillow that is not raw edge, cut four panels.

2. For a double flange pillow that is not raw edge, sew two pieces of fabric together for the front pillow panel, leaving an opening for turning. Repeat for the back panel. Turn the panels right-side up. Press the edges, pressing the opening seam allowances under. Slipstitch the openings closed or edgestitch around each panel.

3. On the front pillow panel, mark the depth of the flange from the seamed outer edge. Layer the front and back panels with wrong sides together. Pin the layers together along the marked line to prevent them from shifting.

4. Stitch on the marked line, leaving an opening for inserting the pillow form or stuffing.

5. Insert the pillow form or stuff the inner area; do not stuff the flange. Topstitch the opening closed, using a zipper foot.

6. If desired, use a wide zigzag stitch and sew flat trim over the flange stitching line.

Style Option

For interest, use a contrasting fabric on the inside of the flanges.

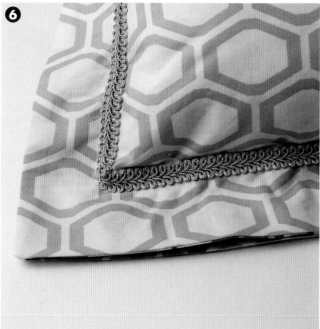

How to Make a Pillow with Contrasting Flange and Overlap Closure

1. Determine the finished size of the stuffed center panel of the pillow. Add 1" (2.5 cm) to the width and length to allow for ½" (1.3 cm) seam allowances; this is the cut width and length of the pillow center front panel. Cut out one pillow center front panel using these measurements, aligning the sides to the fabric grain lines. For the overlapping back panels, add 1" (2.5 cm) to the finished height of the pillow center; this is the cut height of each panel. Divide the width in half and add 3½" (8.8 cm) to this measurement; this is the cut width of each panel. Cut two pillow center back panels using these measurements. Follow the overlapping closure instructions on page 105 to assemble the back panel.

2. Determine the depth of the flange and add 1" (2.5 cm) to the depth measurement; this is the cut width of each flange strip. Double the cut width of the flange and add it to the pillow center cut width; this is the cut length of the top and bottom flange strips. Double the cut width of the flange and add it to the pillow center cut length; this is the cut length of the side flange strips. Using these measurements, cut four top and bottom flange strips and four side flange strips.

3. Mark the center of each edge on the front and back panels. Mark the center of one long edge of each flange strip. Matching the center marks, sew a flange strip to each edge of the front and back center panels, beginning and ending the stitching ½" (1.3 cm) from the corners of the panels.

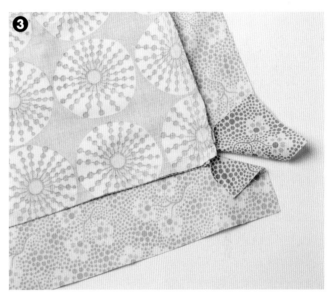

4. To miter each corner, fold the panel in half diagonally, aligning the flange strips. Draw a line from the end of the stitching to the corner and pin; the line should be at a 45-degree angle to the long edges of the flange. Stitch along the line. Trim the excess fabric.

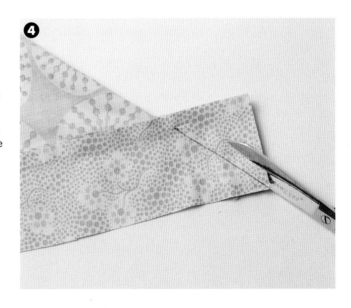

5. Press the flange corners flat. Sew the front panel to the back panel, leaving an opening for turning. Turn right-side out and press. Pin the layers together along the flange seams, making sure the front and back seams are aligned. Stitch the front and back together, stitching in the seam line and leaving an opening parallel with the outer opening.

6. Insert a pillow form or stuff the pillow. Use a zipper foot and stitch the inner opening closed. Slipstitch the outer opening closed or edgestitch around the entire flange.

BOX PILLOWS

Box pillows have fronts and backs that are the same shape and size joined together with a strip of fabric called a boxing strip. The edges of the front and back panels can be finished with welting or you can create a decorative boxing strip to add extra interest to the pillow.

Using the boxing strip technique, you can make a pillow in any shape and in sizes ranging from throw pillows to large floor pillows. Standard pillow forms are available in a limited size range for square and rectangular box edge pillows and fill the cover best when the cover is made 2" (5 cm) smaller in length and width than the form size. You can also make your own pillow form for any shape box edge pillow by cutting muslin pieces the same size as the pillow pieces, sewing them together to make a pillow form, then stuffing them with polyester fiberfill. If you'd like to add a zipper to the boxing strip instead of leaving an opening, see page 124.

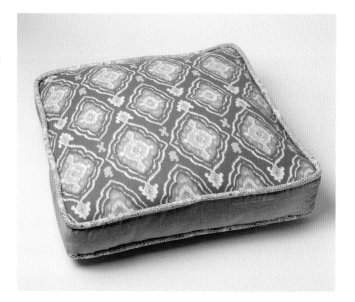

How to Make a Rectangular or Square Box Pillow

1. Determine the finished width, length, and depth of the pillow. Add 1" (2.5 cm) to the width and length for ½" (1.3 cm) seam allowances all around; these are the cut dimensions for the front and back. For the boxing strip cut width, add 1" (2.5 cm) to the determined depth of the pillow.

2. Determine the perimeter of the finished pillow and add 1" (2.5 cm); this is the cut length of the boxing strip. If the boxing strip will need to be pieced, allow 1" (2.5 cm) for each piecing seam.

3. Use the measurements determined in steps 1 and 2 to cut the pillow front and back panels and the boxing strip *Note:* If desired, add welting to the edges of the front and back panels (see page 184).

4. Piece the boxing strip as needed, using ½" (1.3 cm) seam allowances. Sew the short ends of the strip together with right sides facing, to create a continuous loop. Mark both long edges of the boxing strip with the finished lengths of each side of the pillow. Clip into the fabric edge by ⅜" (1 cm) at each mark.

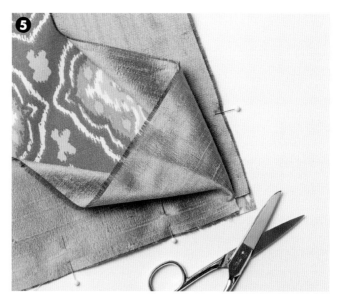

5. Pin the boxing strip to the front pillow panel with right sides and raw edges together, matching the clip marks on the boxing strip to the corners of the panel. The clip marks will spread open.

6. Sew the boxing strip to the panel, using a ½" (1.3 cm) seam allowance. At each corner, stop with the needle down in the fabric, and pivot the fabric. Continue stitching the next side until the strip is sewn to all four sides.

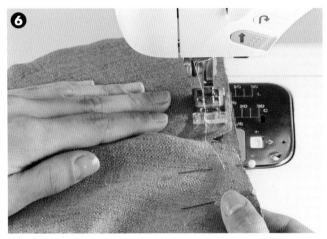

7. Repeat steps 5 and 6 to pin and sew the remaining edge of the boxing strip to the back pillow panel, leaving an opening for turning and stuffing. If you added a zipper closure, unzip the zipper before sewing the second panel in place.

8. Press the seams flat. On each seam allowance, turn back the upper seam allowance and press with the tip of the iron in the crease of the seam. In the area of the opening, press both seam allowances back.

9. Turn the pillow cover right-side out. Square up the corners, using a point turner or other pointed utensil inserted through the opening. Press lightly.

10. Compress and insert the pillow form, making sure the form sits squarely in the cover; add fiberfill in the corners if needed. Or stuff the pillow with fiberfill. Slipstitch the opening closed.

How to Make a Round or Novelty Shape Box Pillow

1. Draw a pattern in the desired shape on paper and cut it out. Use the pattern to cut the front and back pillow panels, adding ½" (1.3 cm) to all edges for seam allowances if you didn't include it in the pattern.

2. Follow step 2 for the rectangular or square box pillow to measure and cut the boxing strip. Piece the boxing strip if necessary, and sew the short ends together to make a continuous loop.

3. Stitch a scant ½" (1.3 cm) from both long edges of the boxing strip. Clip the seam allowance up to, but not into, the stitching at regular intervals where it will be applied to a curved edge.

4. If the pillow shape has inside corners, staystitch on the seam line about 1" (2.5 cm) on each side of the inner corner, pivoting the stitching at the corner. Make a clip up to, but not into, the stitching at each corner.

5. Pin the boxing strip to the front panel with right sides together. Make additional clips if needed for the strip to fit curved edges smoothly or to go around corners neatly.

6. Sew the boxing strip to the front panel, using a ½" (1.3 cm) seam allowance and pivoting at the clips.

7. Repeat to add the back panel, leaving an opening for turning.

8. Press the seams flat. On each seam, turn back the upper seam allowance and press with the tip of the iron in the crease of the seam. In the area of the opening, press both seam allowances back.

9. Turn the pillow cover right-side out. Square up any corners, using a point turner or other pointed utensil inserted through the opening. Press lightly. Stuff the pillow with polyester fiberfill. Slipstitch the opening closed.

How to Add a Zipper to a Boxing Strip

1. Purchase a zipper that is about 2" (5 cm) shorter than one side of a square box edge pillow or one-third the circumference of a round pillow. If you are adding it to a shape like a star, heart, or other design, determine the best location and size for the zipper.

2. Cut a boxing strip for the zipper section 2" (5 cm) wider than the desired finished width of the boxing strip and equal in length to the zipper tape. Cut a boxing strip for the remaining pillow circumference 1" (2.5 cm) wider than the desired finished width and about 6" (15 cm) longer than the remaining circumference.

3. Press the boxing strip for the zipper section in half lengthwise, right sides together. Machine-baste ½" (1.3 cm) from the fold. Cut on the fold; press the seam allowances open.

4. Refer to How to Insert a Conventional Zipper on page 103 to finish applying the zipper.

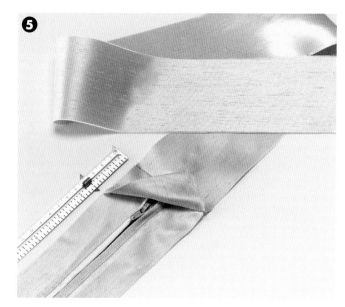

5. Press under 2" (5 cm) on one short end of the boxing strip. Lap the fold over the upper end of the zipper strip to cover the tab. Stitch through all layers 1½" (3.8 cm) from the fold.

6. Trim the remaining end of the boxing strip to the finished pillow circumference plus 1" (2.5 cm) for seam allowances. Pin the cut end to the remaining short edge of the zipper panel, right sides together. Stitch the edges together using a ½" (1.3 cm) seam allowance and stitching slowly over the zipper teeth. Press the seam allowances away from the zipper.

7. Finish the pillow, following the general instructions. Rather than leaving an opening for turning, open the zipper before stitching the final seam.

How to Make a Gathered or Pleated Boxing Strip

A gathered boxing strip can add interest to any pillow. For best results, use a light to medium fabric weight for the boxing strip.

1. Determine the finished width, length, and depth of the pillow. Add 1" (2.5 cm) to the width and length for ½" (1.3 cm) seam allowances all around; these are the cut dimensions for the front and back. Add 1" (2.5 cm) to the pillow depth; this is the cut width of the boxing strip.

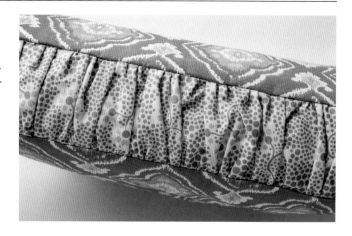

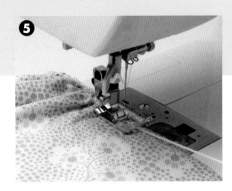

2. Determine the perimeter of the finished pillow. Depending on the amount of fullness you'd like, double or triple this measurement; this is the cut length of the boxing strip. If the boxing strip will need to be pieced, allow 1" (2.5 cm) for each piecing seam.

3. Use the measurements determined in steps 1 and 2 to cut the pillow front and back panels and the boxing strip. *Note:* If desired, add welting to the edges of the front and back panels (page 184).

4. Piece the boxing strip and sew the ends together to make one continuous loop. Mark both long edges of the boxing strip with the finished lengths of each side of the pillow. Clip into the fabric edge ⅜" (1 cm) at each mark.

5. To gather the edges of the boxing strip, cut two pieces of dental floss or narrow cording such as crochet cotton, each equal to the cut length of the boxing strip plus 12" (30.5 cm). Leaving a 6" (15 cm) cord tail, stitch through one end of the cord to secure, then zigzag stitch over the cord ⅜" (1 cm) from one long edge, being careful not to catch the cord in the zigzag stitching. Repeat for the remaining long edge.

6. To pleat the edges of the boxing strip, plan and press equally spaced pleats along the edge, adjusting the pleat depth so the strip fits each edge. Baste across the edges of the pleats to secure.

7. Pin the boxing strip to the front pillow panel at the corners with right sides and raw edges together, matching the clip marks on the boxing strip to the corners of the panel. Do not catch the cord or zigzag stitches in the pins.

8. Pull the cord ends to evenly gather the boxing strip to fit each side of the pillow panel top and knot the cord ends together to secure the gathers. Pin the gathered edge to the pillow panel.

9. Sew the boxing strip to the panel, using a ½" (1.3 cm) seam allowance. At each corner, stop with the needle down in the fabric, and pivot the fabric. Continue stitching the next side until the strip is sewn to all four sides. Remove the cord from under the zigzag stitches.

10. Repeat steps 7 to 9 to pin, gather, and sew the remaining edge of the boxing strip to the back pillow panel, leaving one edge open.

11. Press the seams flat. Then, on each seam, turn back the upper seam allowance and press with the tip of the iron in the crease of the seam. In the area of the opening, press both seam allowances back.

12. Turn the pillow cover right-side up. Square up the corners, using a point turner or other pointed utensil inserted through the opening. Press lightly.

13. Compress and insert the pillow form, making sure the form sits squarely in the cover; add fiberfill in the corners if needed. Or stuff the pillow with fiberfill. Slipstitch the opening closed.

Accent Corners

It can be fun to add a decorative touch to the corners of your finished box pillow when you tack the corners together. You can further embellish them with beads, buttons, or tassels.

MOCK BOX PILLOWS

The mock box pillow has a similar appearance to the box pillow, but the edges are a continuation of the top and bottom panels. Rather than featuring a clearly defined side edge, mock box edge pillows have soft rounded edges. The depth is created by stitching a vertical seam in each corner of the pillow cover, which shortens the pillow width and length. The length of that seam also determines the pillow depth. The larger the pillow, the deeper it can be. For example, a large floor pillow looks attractive with a depth of 6" (15 cm), while a smaller sofa pillow looks better with a depth of 2½" to 3" (6.3 to 7.5 cm). The perimeter seam circles the pillow halfway between the front and back and can incorporate welting, if desired.

The chart below shows the cut sizes needed for the finished sizes of mock box pillows that will fit standard pillow forms. Cut sizes include ½" (1.3 cm) seam allowances.

Cutting Guide for Mock Box Pillows

Finished Size	Depth	Cut Size	Form Size
10" × 10"	2"	13" × 13"	12" × 12"
(25.5 × 25.5 cm)	(5 cm)	(33 × 33 cm)	(30.5 × 30.5 cm)
11½" × 11½"	2½"	15" × 15"	14" × 14"
(29.3 × 29.3 cm)	(6.5 cm)	(38 × 38 cm)	(35.5 × 35.5 cm)
13" × 13"	3"	17" × 17"	16" × 16"
(33 × 33 cm)	(7.5 cm)	(43 × 43 cm)	(40.5 × 40.5 cm)
14½" × 14½"	3½"	19" × 19"	18" × 18"
(36.8 × 36.8 cm)	(9 cm)	(48.5 × 48.5 cm)	(46 × 46 cm)
16" × 16"	4"	21" × 21"	20" × 20"
(40.5 × 40.5 cm)	(10 cm)	(53.5 × 53.5 cm)	(51 × 51 cm)
19" × 19"	5"	25" × 25"	24" × 24"
(48.5 × 48.5 cm)	(12.7 cm)	(63.5 × 63.5 cm)	(61 × 61 cm)
24" × 24"	6"	31" × 31"	30" × 30"
(61 × 61 cm)	(15 cm)	(78.5 × 78.5 cm)	(76 × 76 cm)

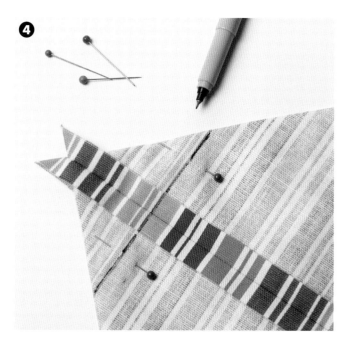

How to Make a Mock Box Pillow

1. Cut out the pillow front and back, aligning the sides to the fabric grain lines. Refer to the chart on page 126 for cut size guidelines.

2. Sew the pillow front to the back with right sides together, using a ½" (1.3 cm) seam allowance and pivoting at the corners. Leave an opening on one lengthwise-grain side for stuffing the pillow. Press the seam allowances open.

3. Pull the front and back away from each other at one corner, and refold the fabric so a new corner is formed with the seams in the center. Pin through the seams to make sure they are aligned.

4. Measure along the seam and mark a point a distance from the corner that equals half the desired pillow depth. Draw a line through the point, perpendicular to the seam, from fold to fold. The length of the line should equal the total desired pillow depth.

5. Stitch along the marked line and remove the pins. Do not cut the excess fabric. Repeat for each corner.

6. Turn the pillow cover right-side up. Square up the corners, using a point turner or other pointed utensil inserted through the opening.
Press lightly.

7. Compress and insert the pillow form, making sure the form sits squarely in the cover; add fiberfill in the corners if needed. Or stuff the pillow with fiberfill. Slipstitch the opening closed.

How to Make a Bolster Pillow with Drawstring Ends

1. Measure the length and circumference of the pillow form or determine the length and circumference if you want to make a form. Cut a rectangle of fabric with the width equal to the circumference of the form plus 1" (2.5 cm) and the length equal to the length of the form plus the diameter plus 1½" (3.8 cm) for the casings.

2. Press under ¼" (6 mm), then ½" (1.3 cm) on each short end of the fabric rectangle for the casings. Unfold the ends. Fold the fabric in half lengthwise, right sides together. Stitch the long edges together using a ½" (1.3 cm) seam allowance, beginning and ending with back-stitches ¾" (2 cm) from each end. Press the seam allowance open.

BOLSTER PILLOWS

Bolster pillows, also called neckroll pillows, are cylindrical and are both useful and decorative. As the name implies, they are comfortable when placed behind the neck or back. For decorating, longer versions look nice placed in front of pillows on a bed and all sizes and lengths add an attractive shape variation to a group of square or rectangular pillows. The most basic bolster pillow is made with a rectangle of fabric sewn into a cylinder and drawn closed at each end with a drawstring in a casing. You can also extend the ends of the cylinder and tie the ends with ribbon cording or a chair tie so it resembles a piece of wrapped candy. For a more tailored version, you can cap the ends with round panels and optional welting. An oversize, flattened version of a bolster pillow is also ideal—and comfy—for use as a body pillow.

Bolster forms are available in several sizes or you can make your own in a custom size.

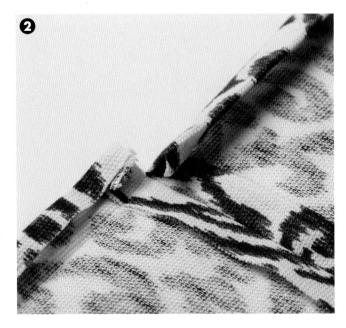

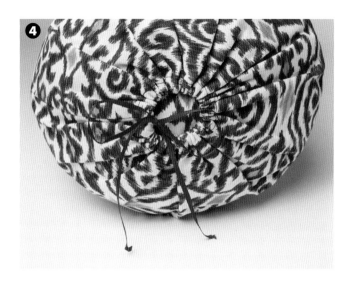

3. Refold the casings. Edgestitch along the inner folds; reinforce the stitches at the openings. Turn the bolster cover right-side out.

4. Thread narrow cording or ribbon through the casings, leaving the ends long enough to tie. Insert the bolster form. Draw up the cording or ribbon and tie securely. If the form isn't completely covered, place a circle of matching fabric over each end before tying the cords or ribbon.

How to Make a Candy Wrapper Bolster

1. Cut a rectangle of fabric with the width equal to the circumference of the bolster form plus 1" (2.5 cm) and the length equal to the length of the bolster form plus three times the diameter.

2. Press under ¼" (6 mm) on each short end of the rectangle, then unfold. Fold the fabric in half lengthwise, right sides together. Stitch the long edges together using a ½" (1.3 cm) seam allowance, beginning and ending with backstitches ¾" (2 cm) from each end.

3. Refold the ¼" (6 mm) on the short ends. Fold the ends under half the diameter of the bolster. Edgestitch along the inner folds, reinforcing the stitching at the openings. Stitch again ½" (1.3 cm) from each inner fold to form a casing.

4. Thread narrow cord or ribbon through the casings, leaving the ends long enough to tie. Turn the bolster cover right-side out. Insert the bolster form. Draw up the cording and tie the ends together securely. Tuck the cord ends into the openings.

5. On the outside of the pillow, tie decorative cording, ribbon, or a tasseled tieback around each gathered end, if desired.

How to Make a Tailored Bolster Pillow

1. Cut a rectangle of fabric with a width equal to the circumference of the pillow form, plus 1" (2.5 cm), and the length equal to the length of the pillow form, plus 1" (2.5 cm). Cut two circles of fabric for the ends with the diameter equal to the diameter of the bolster form plus 1" (2.5 cm).

2. Fold the rectangle in half with right sides together. Sew the edges that are the same length as the bolster plus 1" (2.5 cm) together, using a ½" (1.3 cm) seam allowance. Leave an opening in the center of the seam that is long enough for turning the cover and inserting the bolster form.

3. Divide each end of the cylinder into fourths and mark with pins. Stitch a scant ½" (1.3 cm) from the outer edge of each end. Clip into the fabric every ½" (1.3 cm) up to, but not into, the stitching line. Divide the edge of each end circle in fourths and mark with pins.

4. On the right side of each end circle, apply self-adhesive, double-sided basting tape around the outer edge. Remove the paper backing. With right sides together and raw edges even, adhere a circle to each end of the center, matching the quarter marks and easing the clipped edge onto the basting tape. With the cylinder facing up, stitch each end circle in place using a ½" (1.3 cm) seam allowance.

5. If desired, use fabric glue to apply trim with a decorative heading around each end of the pillow, or hand stitch it in place.

How to Make a Bolster Form

1. Determine the length of your bolster pillow; this will be the cut width of the batting. Cut a rectangle of batting 1 yd (1 m) long in the determined width.

2. Roll the batting with the desired firmness until it is the desired diameter. If you roll it loosely it will be softer. Tightly rolled batting will result in a smaller, firmer roll. Trim the excess batting or add more as needed to achieve the desired size. Pin the edge in place.

3. Whipstitch the edge of the batting to the roll.

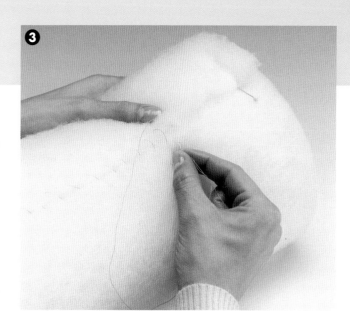

How to Make a Body Bean

If you're looking for extra comfort while you sleep, consider making a body bean pillow. These soft, huggable pillows conform naturally to your body as you sleep. They are cylindrical and made in the same manner as a bolster pillow. Cotton, soft knit, fleece, or flannel fabrics are ideal for making these pillows.

1. Decide the length of the pillow based on the height of the person who will be using it. Generally the length of an adult's pillow is 66" (167.7 cm) and the length of a teen's pillow is 54" (137.2 cm). A standard diameter is 10" to 12" (25 to 30 cm).

2. To determine the length of the fabric rectangle to cut, add 1" (2.5 cm) for seam allowances to the desired pillow length. To determine the width, multiply the desired diameter by 3.14 and add 1" (2.5 cm) for seam allowances. Cut one rectangle using these measurements. For the ends, cut two circles, each equal to the pillow diameter plus 1" (2.5 cm) for seam allowances.

3. Fold the rectangle in half lengthwise with right sides together. Sew the long edges together, using a ½" (1.3 cm) seam allowance. Leave an opening in the center of the seam that is long enough for turning the cover and stuffing the pillow. Press the seam allowance open.

4. Stitch a scant ½" (1.3 cm) from the outer edge of each end of the cylinder. Clip into the fabric every ½" (1.3 cm) up to, but not into, the stitching line.

5. With right sides together, pin a circle to each end of the cylinder, aligning the raw edges. Sew the circles to the ends.

6. Turn the cover right-side out. Stuff with polyester fiberfill to the desired fullness; use less fiberfill for a more "squishable" pillow.

7. Slipstitch the opening closed.

THE COMPLETE PHOTO GUIDE TO SLIPCOVERS, PILLOWS & BEDDING

Bean Bag Chair

Kids and adults alike love bean bag chairs. Nothing beats these squishy chairs for comfort when you want to relax and read, or settle in and watch a good movie. Simply snuggle down into the chair and its shape conforms to your body. Because they invite wear and tear, be sure to use a medium-weight to heavyweight fabric such as canvas, denim, wide wale corduroy, outdoor fabrics, vinyl, faux fur, or upholstery fabric, and ensure stable seams by using heavy thread.

For extra durability, the bean bag chair consists of a muslin inner lining, which holds lightweight polystyrene pellets, and an outer cover. Both are zippered, making the inner lining easy to fill and removable for laundering or dry cleaning. Patterns are provided for both an adult size and a child size on page 135. The instructions are the same for an adult's chair and a child's chair, only the sizes of the pieces are different.

YOU WILL NEED

Adult's chair

- 5 yd (4.6 m) fabric 44" to 48" (111.8 to 121.9 cm) wide or 3½ yd (3.2 m) fabric 54" (137.2 cm) wide for the outer chair
- muslin (same amount as for outer cover)
- 22" (55.9 cm) zipper
- 6 cubic ft (1.8 cubic m) polystyrene pellets

Child's chair

- 3 yd (2.7 m) fabric 44" to 48" (111.8 to 121.9 cm) wide or 2½ yd (2.3 m) of fabric 54" (137.2 cm) wide for the outer chair
- muslin (same amount as for outer cover)
- 18" (45.7 cm) zipper
- 4 cubic ft (1.2 cubic m) polystyrene pellets

How to Make a Bean Bag Chair

1. To make either size chair, place tracing paper over a 1" (2.5 cm) grid, and draw the pattern using the illustration on page 135 as a guide.

2. For the chair bottom pattern, fold a piece of tracing paper in half. Mark the center of the folded edge. Measuring from the center, draw an arc with a 12" (30.5 cm) radius for an adult's chair or a 10" (25.5 cm) radius for a child's chair. Unfold the paper; mark a line ½" (1.3 cm) from the fold. Cut on the marked line. Discard the smaller section of the circle and use the larger section for cutting.

3. Use the side panel pattern to cut six side panels from the outer fabric and six from muslin. Use the bottom pattern to cut two pieces from the outer fabric and two from muslin. From both the fabric and muslin, cut one circle with a 5½" (14 cm) radius for the top of an adult chair or a 4½" (11.3 cm) radius for the top of a child's chair.

4. Pin the straight edges of the chair bottom pieces together with right sides facing. Machine-baste the edges together, using a ½" (1.3 cm) seam allowance and stitching 1" (2.5 cm) at each end of the seam with a regular stitch length.

5. Press the seam open. Center the zipper right side down over the seam allowances with the zipper teeth on the seam line. Glue-baste or use basting tape to secure the zipper tapes. Stitch down each side of the zipper ¼" (6 mm) from the zipper teeth. Remove the basting stitches.

6. With right sides facing, use a ½" (1.3 cm) seam allowance and sew the side panels together, leaving the last seam unstitched. Press the seam allowances to one side, pressing all in the same direction. On the right side, topstitch ⅜" (1 cm) from the seams, securing the seam allowances. Sew the remaining seam, press, and topstitch.

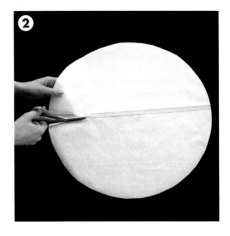

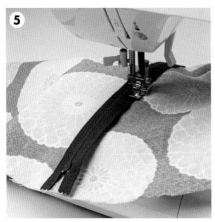

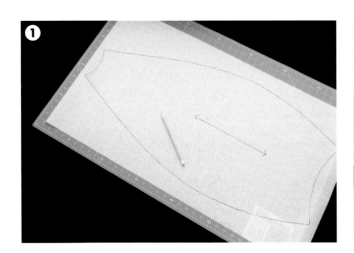

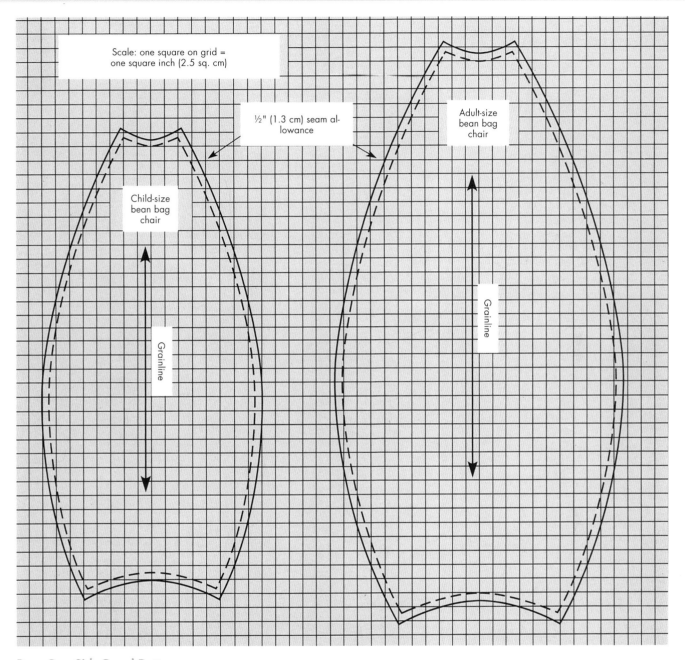

Bean Bag Side Panel Patterns

7. Staystitch the upper edge of the chair a scant ½" (1.3 cm) from the edge. Clip the seam allowance up to (but not into) the stitching at ½" (1.3 cm) intervals.

8. Divide the outer edge of the top circle into six equal parts and mark with pins. With right sides facing, pin the top circle to the top of the chair, matching the pin marks on the top to the seams on the chair. Sew the top in place, using a ½" (1.3 cm) seam allowance. Press the seam allowances toward the sides. Topstitch ⅜" (1 cm) from the top seam to secure the seam allowances.

10. Repeat steps 7 and 8 to attach and topstitch the bottom of the bean bag, leaving the zipper partially open during assembly to turn the bean bag right-side out.

11. Repeat steps 4 through 10 to assemble the muslin lining. Insert the lining into the outer cover. Fill the bag with polystyrene pellets. Close the zippers.

Tuffet

Tuffets come in a variety of diameters and heights ranging from over-sized floor pillows to taller versions that are ottoman height. You can use them for extra seating or for a comfy place to rest your feet. Use medium- to heavyweight decorator fabric and stuff the tuffet very firmly so it will maintain its shape when sat upon. The featured tuffet has a 20" (50.8 cm) diameter and is 17" (43.2 cm) high, but you can easily adapt the instructions to other sizes.

YOU WILL NEED

- decorator fabric
- beaded trim and gimp (optional)
- fusible web tape (optional)
- polyester fiberfill
- upholstery needle

How to Make a Tuffet

1. Decide the height and diameter of your tuffet. To determine the sizes of the top, bottom, and sides, multiply the diameter by 3.14 to determine the circumference. For the side panel, plan a rectangle with a height equal to the tuffet height, plus 1" (2.5 cm) for seam allowances. For the side panel width, add 1" (2.5 cm) for seam allowances to the circumference; if the measurement exceeds the fabric width, plan to cut and piece two panels, adding 1" (2.5 cm) for each seam. For the top and bottom panels, plan two circles, each with a diameter to match the tuffet diameter plus 1" (2.5 cm) for seam allowances.

2. Cut the sides, top, and bottom as determined in step 1 from the decorator fabric. If you are piecing the side panel, match the print at one seam line.

3. If needed, sew the side panel pieces together, matching the print.

4. Fold the side panel in half crosswise with right sides together. Sew the short edges together, using a ½" (1.3 cm) seam allowance and leaving a 6" (15 cm) opening in the seam for turning and stuffing.

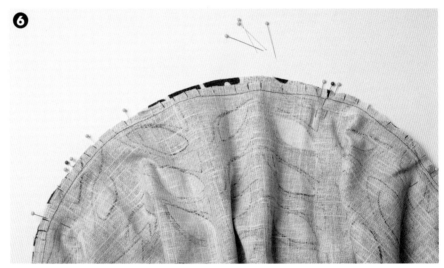

5. Stitch around the top and bottom edges of the side panel a scant ½" (1.3 cm) from the edge. Clip the seam allowance up to, but not into, the stitching at ½" (1.3 cm) intervals.

6. Fold the side panel in fourths width-wise and mark the top and bottom of each fold with a pin. Fold the top and bottom circles in fourths and mark each fold with a pin. Matching the quarter marks, pin the top to the sides.

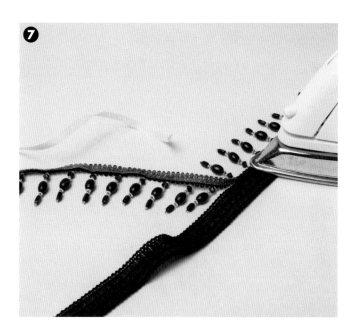

7. With the side panel up, sew the sides to the top. If you are adding beaded trim and gimp as shown on the featured tuffet, cut a length of each trim that is equal to the perimeter of the tuffet, plus 2" (5 cm). Use fusible web tape to adhere the bead trim header to the wrong side of the gimp trim.

8. Sew the gimp trim around the top edge of the tuffet, aligning the top edge of the trim with the seam line. Stitch both edges of the trim in place. Overlap the ends and turn under the top end; stitch in place.

9. Sew the bottom to the sides. Turn right-side out and press.

10. Stuff the tuffet very firmly with polyester fiberfill. Slip stitch the opening closed using a doubled strand of thread. Use a long upholstery needle to adjust the stuffing until the tuffet sides and top are smooth and it is rounded evenly.

BEDDING

There's no better place to begin and end the day than in a beautifully decorated bedroom. It's easy to achieve when you use beautiful fabrics and trims to make duvet covers, bedspreads, or coverlets to cover the bed. Add eye-catching pillow shams and a bed skirt, and you have a designer-looking ensemble to enjoy.

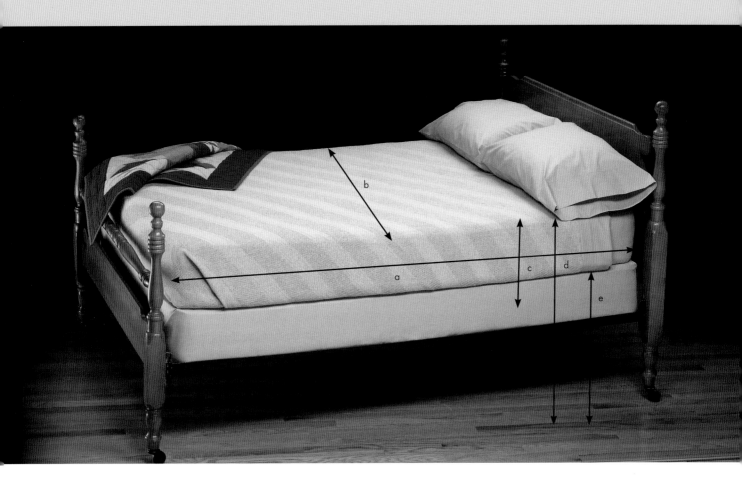

Measurements

One key to successful sewing for the bedroom is to measure the bed so the pieces fit accurately. No matter what size the bed is, the measurements will vary depending on the model or manufacturer. Take the measurements over the blankets and sheets that will be used on the bed to ensure a correct fit. Referring to the photo above, measure the length of the bed (a), and the width of the bed (b). Also refer to the Bedding Size Chart (opposite) to plan your ensemble.

Duvets and coverlets hang 1" to 4" (2.5 to 10 cm) below the mattress on the sides and at the foot of the bed. Determine the drop length of the duvet or coverlet by measuring from the top of the bed to the desired length (c).

When measuring for a full-length bedspread, measure the drop length from the top of the mattress to the floor (d); then subtract ½" (1.3 cm) for clearance.

When measuring for a bed skirt, measure the drop length from the top of the box spring to the floor (e); then subtract ½" (1.3 cm) for clearance.

Bed pillows and comforters also vary in size from standard measurements. For best results, measure them from seam to seam in each direction before making pillow shams or duvet covers.

BEDDING SIZE CHART

Size	Mattress	Bedspread	Coverlet	Comforter
Twin	39" x 75" (99 x 190.5 cm)	81" x 116" (205.7 x 294.6 cm)	63" x 107" (160 x 271.8 cm)	65"–69" x 88"–90" (165–175.3 cm x 223.5–228.6 cm)
Full	54" x 75" (137 x 190.5 cm)	96" x 116" (243.8 x 294.6 cm)	78" x 107" (198 x 271.8 cm)	80"–84" x 88"–90" (203.2–213.4 cm x 223.5–228.6 cm)
Queen	60" x 80" (152.4 x 203.2 cm)	102" x 121" (259 x 307.3 cm)	84" x 112" (213.4 x 284.5 cm)	86"–90" x 94"–95" 218.4–228.6 cm x 238.8–241.3 cm)
King	76" x 80" (193 x 203.2 cm)	114" x 121" (289.6 x 307.3 cm)	102" x 112" (259 x 284.5 cm)	106"–110" x 96"–98" (269–279.4 cm x 243.8–248.9 cm)

PILLOW SIZE CHART

Pillow	Sizes
Standard	20" x 26" (50.8 x 66 cm)
Queen	20" x 30" (50.8 x 76.2 cm)
King	20" x 36" (50.8 x 91.4 cm)
Euro	22" x 22" (55.9 x 55.9 cm)

Duvet Covers

One of the easiest ways to give any bed a fresh, new look is with a duvet cover. Not only are they quick and easy to make, duvet covers are also usually made with lightweight fabric or even sheets, making them more of a budget-friendly option than using more expensive decorator fabrics. Because a duvet cover is used to cover a comforter, it is easily removed for laundering or for changing to suit your mood.

YOU WILL NEED

- decorator fabric or flat sheets
- double-sided basting tape
- buttons or hook-and-loop tape (optional)
- 8 strips of ribbon or narrow twill tape, if adding corner ties
- cording, if adding welting or twisted cord edge embellishment

WHAT YOU NEED TO KNOW

A duvet cover is made with two panels of fabric sewn together along the sides and one end. The other end has a closure that is tied, buttoned, or closed with hook and loop tape. You can also create a faced open end with ties or an overlap on the underside for a hidden closure. The closure is usually at the foot end of the duvet cover, unless it is intended as a decorative element for the head end.

Unless you are using sheets or very wide fabric, it is necessary to piece the duvet cover panels. Cut a full fabric width for the center panel. For the side panels, cut the fabric panel in half lengthwise and sew a half panel to each side of the center panel. To match a print, cut the side panel length a full print repeat length longer.

Edge treatments such as welting, a flange, or a contrasting border add a designer touch. A flange added to a duvet cover extends past the finished size needed to cover the comforter. The flange depth can range from 1" to 3" (2.5 to 7.5 cm), depending on the look you want. You can also choose to piece the top with coordinating borders or panels. To prevent the comforter from shifting inside the cover, you may want to add inside ties.

How to Make a Duvet Cover with Hemmed Closure

1. Refer to the Bedding Size Chart on page 143 to determine the finished size of the duvet cover. A finished cover with a hemmed closure needs to be at least 1½" (3.8 cm) longer than the comforter it will cover. If piecing is necessary, use one full fabric width for the center panel, and two equal partial widths for the side panels. Be sure to match the fabric print at the seam lines before cutting the length of the side panels. To match the print, press under ½" (1.3 cm) on each long edge of the center panel. Match the folded edge to the print design on the side panel; pin in place or fuse together with double-sided basting tape, as shown.

2. Sew the side panels to the center panel. Cut the side panel length even with the center panel. Repeat for the back panels.

3. For a duvet cover with a button or hook–and-loop tape closure, cut the fabric for the duvet cover front and back panels 1" (2.5 cm) wider and 3½" (7.5 cm) longer than the finished duvet size.

4. With right sides facing, use a ½" (1.3 cm) seam allowance and sew the panels together along the side and bottom edges. Turn right-side out and press. Press the upper edges under 1" (2.5 cm), then press under 1" (2.5 cm) again to make a doubled hem. Topstitch the hem in place close to the inner fold.

5. For a hook-and-loop tape closure, cut a strip of hook-and-loop tape 2" (5 cm) shorter than the finished width. Center the loop side of the strip on the underside of the front panel hem and edgestitch in place. Center the hook side on the underside of the back panel and edgestitch in place.

6. For a buttoned closure, mark a buttonhole placement in the center of the top panel hemmed edge. Mark buttonholes spaced 10" (25.5 cm) apart across the edge in each direction. Stitch the buttonholes. Sew buttons to the hemmed edge of the back panel to correspond with the buttonholes.

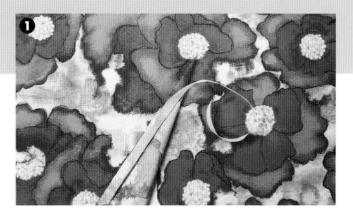

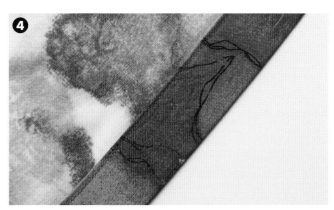

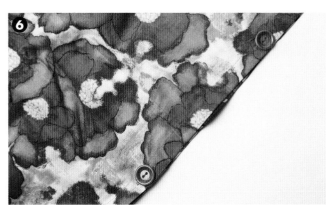

How to Make a Duvet Cover with Tied Closure

1. Refer to the Bedding Size Chart on page 143 to determine the finished size of the duvet cover. A tied closure needs to be at least 1" (2.5 cm) longer than the comforter it will cover. If piecing is necessary, use one full fabric width for the center panel, and two equal partial widths for the side panels. Be sure to match the fabric print at the seam lines before cutting the panels.

2. Cut the fabric for the front and back panels 1" (2.5 cm) wider and longer than the finished cover. For the inside facing, cut two strips of fabric 6" (15 cm) wide, each 1" (2.5 cm) longer than the cover finished width. For the ties, plan to place ties across the width of the opening at 12" to 14" (30.5 to 35.5 cm) intervals. Cut two 1½" x 10" (3.8 x 25.5 cm) strips of fabric for each set of ties or plan to use strips of ribbon.

3. With right sides facing, use a ½" (1.3 cm) seam allowance and sew the front and back panels together along the side and bottom edges. Turn right-side out and press.

❹

4. If you are making fabric ties, press one short end on each strip under ½" (1.3 cm). Press the strip in half with wrong sides together. Open it and press the edges under to meet at the center fold. Press in half again, encasing the raw edges. Edgestitch the open edges closed.

5. On the top edge of the front panel right side, evenly space and pin the ties across the edge with raw edges even, beginning and ending 4" (10 cm) from each side edge. If the duvet cover will have a flange edge, begin 4" (10 cm) from the marked flange line.

❻

6. Repeat for the back panel, aligning the tie placements with the front panel.

7. Use a ½" (1.3 cm) seam allowance and sew the short edges of the facing strips together with right sides facing. Finish one long edge with serging or zigzag stitches. Place the facing strip along the top edge of the cover, aligning sides and raw edges. Sew the facing in place. Press the facing to the inside of the cover and tack the edge in place at the sides. Topstitch ¼" (6 mm) from the seam.

❼

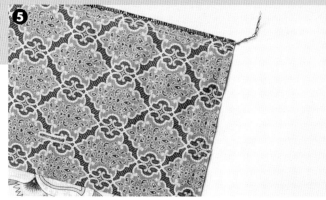

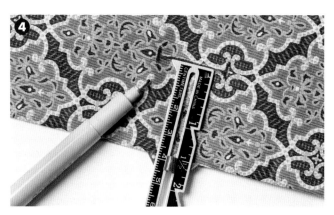

How to Make a Duvet Cover with Horizontal Lapped Closure

1. Refer to the Bedding Size Chart on page 143 to determine the finished size of the duvet cover. If piecing is necessary, use one full fabric width for the center panel, and two equal partial widths for the side panels. Be sure to match the fabric print at the seam lines before cutting the length of the side panels.

2. Cut the fabric for the front and back panels 1" (2.5 cm) wider and longer than the finished cover, piecing if needed. For the overlapping band, cut one upper edge band 13" (33 cm) wide and 1" (2.5 cm) longer than the finished cover width.

3. Press the upper edge band in half lengthwise with wrong sides together. Baste the raw edges together.

4. Mark a buttonhole in the center of the band, 1½" (3.8 cm) from the folded edge. Mark buttonholes spaced 8" (20 cm) apart across the edge in each direction. Stitch the buttonholes.

5. Pin the band to the top edge of the front panel with right sides together, and raw edges even. Sew the long edges together, then finish with zigzag stitches or serging. Baste the side edges of the band to the front panel.

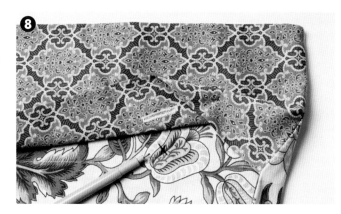

6. Press the top edge of the back panel under 3" (7.5 cm) and topstitch in place.

7. Pin the back panel to the front panel with right sides together and the hemmed top edge of the back panel 3" (7.5 cm) below the top edge of the front panel. Use a ½" (1.3 cm) seam allowance and sew the front and back panels together along the side and bottom edges. Trim the corners.

8. Turn the band to the outside over the back. Mark the button placements and sew buttons to the marks.

How to Add Inside Corner Ties

1. Cut 8 strips of ribbon or narrow twill tape 6" (15 cm) long.

2. Tack a strip of ribbon to each corner of the comforter.

3. Turn the duvet cover wrong-side out. Tack a strip of ribbon to each bottom corner and each side of the top edge at the side seam. For a hemmed closure, sew the ribbon to the side seam just below the hem.

4. Tie the comforter to the cover at the corners. Turn the cover right-side out over the comforter.

Prevent Shifting

For queen- and king- size duvets, it is also helpful to tack ribbons to the halfway points on all sides to keep the comforter from shifting.

How to Add Welting or Twisted Cord to the Edges

Welting or twisted cord with a lip adds a professional-looking finish and defines the edges of a duvet cover.

1. Follow the basic construction instructions to cut and piece the front and back panels of the cover (steps 1 and 2 on page 146). If desired, round the bottom corners for smoother trim application.

2. On the front panel, measure the edges and add 6" (15 cm) to the total measurement to determine the length of the welting to cover. Refer to pages 184 to 186 to cut bias strips and cover the cording. For twisted cord, cut the determined length, plus 6" (15 cm).

3. Use a zipper foot and begin at the top of one side edge on the front panel. Sew the trim to the edge, aligning the trim lip with the fabric edge.

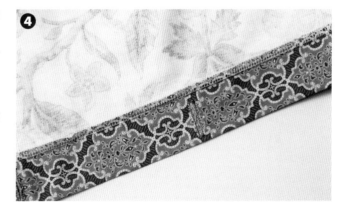

4. Finish the duvet cover, following the instructions for the type of cover you are making. Securely baste or serge the trim edge in place before finishing the upper edge.

How to make a Duvet Cover with a Flange

1. Refer to the basic construction instructions on page 146. Determine the finished size of the duvet cover (excluding the flange) and the depth of the flange.

2. Double the flange depth and add it to the finished width of the duvet cover. Add the finished flange depth to the finished length of the cover. These are the cut measurements for the front and back panels. Refer to the instructions for closure options to add any additional length to the cut panels as needed. Cut and piece the panels.

3. Sew the panels together along the side and bottom edges. Turn right-side out and press. Using a disappearing fabric marker or chalk, mark the flange depth on the side and bottom edges of the front panel.

4. Finish the upper edges of the panels with the desired closure option up to the flange marks. Press the flange edges under to align with the finished opening edges.

5. Pin the layers together across the marked flange line. Stitch along the line. Edgestitch the pressed-under flange edges together at the top edges of the cover.

How to Add a Contrasting Border

A contrasting border is only added to the side and bottom edges of the duvet cover front panel. Unlike a flange, which extends beyond the body of the cover, an edge border is part of the panel that covers the comforter.

1. Determine the finished and cut sizes of the duvet cover and decide on a closure style. Cut and piece the back panels following the basic construction instructions on page 146.

2. For the front panel, decide how deep you'd like to make the border. Subtract this depth from each side and the end of the finished duvet cover size from step 1 to determine the finished size of the main front panel. The length of the finished side borders will each be equal to the length of the main panel. The finished end border will be equal in depth to the finished width of the main panels and side border.

3. Use the measurements in step 2 to cut the main front panel (piecing if needed), two side border strips, and one end border strip, adding ½" (1.3 cm) seam allowances to all edges when cutting.

4. Beginning at the top edge, sew a border strip to each side edge of the front panel. Sew the bottom border to the edge.

5. Refer to the basic construction instructions on page 146 to assemble and finish the duvet cover.

How to Add a Ruffle

Like a flange, ruffles are added only to the side and end edges of the duvet cover.

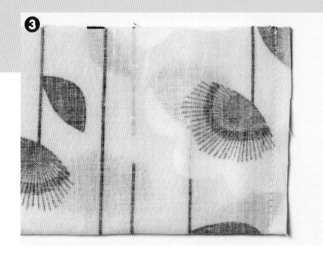

1. Determine the finished size of the duvet cover and decide on a closure style. Cut and piece the front and back panels following the basic construction instructions on page 146.

2. Cut fabric strips for the ruffle on the crosswise or lengthwise grain, with the combined length of the strips two to three times the distance to be ruffled. The width of the strips should be twice the finished depth of the ruffle plus 1" (2.5 cm) for seam allowances.

3. Sew the short edges of the ruffle strips together with right sides facing, using a ¼" (6 mm) seam allowance. Press the seam allowances open. Fold the ruffle strip in half lengthwise with right sides facing. Stitch across each end, using a ¼" (6 mm) seam allowance.

4. Turn the ruffle right-side out and press the ends. Press the ruffle strip in half lengthwise.

5. Zigzag stitch over heavy thread or cord ⅜" (1 cm) from the raw edges. For more control when adjusting gathers, zigzag stitch over a second cord, within the seam allowance, ¼" (6 mm) from the first cord.

6. Divide the distance to be ruffled (side and bottom edges) on the duvet cover front panel into fourths and mark with pins. Divide the ruffle strip into fourths and mark with pins. With raw edges even, match the pin marks and pin the ruffle to the front panel at the marks. Pull the gathering cord or cords to evenly gather the ruffle to fit the panel and pin in place.

7. Stitch the ruffle strip to the panel ⅜" (1 cm) from the edge. Sew the front and back panels together, using a ½" (1.3 cm) seam allowance.

Pillow Shams

Pillow shams add the perfect finishing touch to your bedding ensemble when designed to complement the duvet cover or quilted coverlet. Make them in matching or coordinating fabric to cover any bed pillow from a standard size to a Euro size (see the Pillow Sizes chart on page 143).

WHAT YOU NEED TO KNOW

As decorative elements of the bedding ensemble, pillow shams are designed to cover the bed pillows stylishly yet afford easy removal for sleeping. Basic shams have a simple overlapping closure on the back. You can add buttons and buttonholes or hook-and-loop tape to the overlapping edges if desired. You can also close shams with several decorative options, including buttons on the front or ties.

Edge treatments, such as a flange, welting, twisted cord, ruffles, or fringe can also be applied, and usually reflect the same treatment used for the duvet cover.

YOU WILL NEED

- decorator fabric
- cotton batting
- lining
- buttons or hook-and-loop tape, optional
- disappearing fabric marker or chalk, if making flanged sham

How to Make a Basic Pillow Sham

1. Refer to the Pillow Size Chart on page 143 or measure the pillow height and width from seam to seam.

2. For the sham front, cut a panel that is 1" (2.5 cm) longer and wider than the pillow size. For the back, determine half the width and add 3" (7.5 cm) to the measurement; cut two panels in this width, each 1" (2.5 cm) longer than the pillow height. Also cut one cotton batting piece and one lining piece the same size as the front panel.

3. Layer the lining piece, batting, and fabric right-side up, with edges even; baste the layers together.

4. Refer to the instructions for adding welting (pillows, page 107), or ruffles (shams, page 159) to the edges of the front panel, if desired.

5. On the back panels, press under ¼" (6 mm) on the edges that will overlap. Press each edge under ¼" (6 mm) again to make a doubled hem. Topstitch close to the inner fold.

6. Place the front panel right-side up. Place the back panels right-side down on the front panel, overlapping the edges until the back panel is the same width as the front. Pin the layers together.

7. Sew the panels together around the outside edges, using a ½" (1.3 cm) seam allowance. Turn right-side out and press. Insert pillow.

How to Make a Flanged Sham

1. Cut pieces for the sham following instructions for flanged pillows (page 118). Also cut one piece of low-loft batting and one piece of lining in the combined dimensions of the finished front panel and flanges.

2. Baste the batting to the wrong side of the front panel.

3. Refer to steps 5 and 6 of the basic sham instructions to layer the front and back panels and stitch the edges.

5. Use a disappearing fabric marker or chalk to mark the flange stitching line 2½" (6.3 cm) from the edges.

6. Pin the layers together along the marked line, then top stitch along the line.

Secure Closure

If desired, add evenly spaced buttons and buttonholes or hook-and-loop tape to the overlapping edges to make a secured closure. For a secured closure, add 2" (5 cm) to the cut width of the back panels instead of 3" (7.5 cm).

How to Make a Sham with Contrasting Flange

1. Measure the pillow length and width. Add 1" (2.5 cm) to each measurement to determine the cut dimensions of the sham body front panel.

2. For the sham body front, cut a panel that is 1" (2.5 cm) longer and wider than the pillow size. For the back, determine half the width and add 3" (7.5 cm) to the measurement; cut two panels in this width, each 1" (2.5 cm) longer than the pillow height. Also cut one cotton batting piece and one lining piece the same size as the front panel.

3. Determine the depth of the flange and add 1" (2.5 cm) to the depth measurement; this is the cut width of each flange strip. Double the cut width of the flange and add it to the sham body cut width; this is the cut length of the top and bottom flange strips. Double the cut width of the flange and add it to the flange body cut length; this is the cut length of the side flange strips. Cut four top and bottom flange strips and four side flange strips, using these measurements.

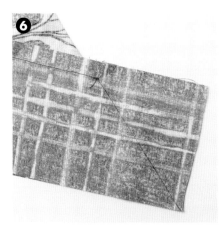

4. Follow the basic pillow sham instructions on page 156 to hem and overlap the back panels to match the size of the front panel. Baste the top and bottom of the overlapping edges together.

5. Mark the center of each edge on the front and back panels. Mark the center of one long edge of each flange strip. Matching the center marks, sew a flange strip to each edge of the front and back center panels, beginning and ending the stitching ½" (1.3 cm) from the corners of the panels.

6. To miter each corner, fold the panel in half diagonally, aligning the flange strips. Draw a line from the end of the stitching to the corner and pin; the line should be at a 45-degree angle to the long edges of the flange. Stitch along the line. Trim the excess fabric

7. Press the flange corners flat. Sew the front panel to the back panel, leaving an opening for turning. Turn right-side out and press. Pin the layers together along the flange seams, making sure the front and back seams are aligned. Stitch the front and back together by stitching in the seam line.

How to Make a Sham with Ruffled Edge

1. Follow the basic sham instructions on page 156 to cut the front and back panels. Layer the lining piece, batting, and fabric right-side up, with edges even; baste the layers together.

2. Decide the width of the ruffle. Double the width and add 1" (2.5 cm) for seam allowances to determine the cut width of the strips. The combined length of the strips should be double the circumference of the sham. Cut the number of strips needed, allowing for ¼" (6 mm) seam allowances. Sew the strips together to make a continuous circle.

3. Follow steps 3 through 7 for a duvet cover ruffle on page 153, to gather the ruffle and sew it to the edge of the front sham panel.

4. Follow the basic sham instructions to assemble the front and back panels.

5. Turn right-side out and press.

How to Make a Tied Closure

1. Follow the basic sham instructions on page 156 to cut the pillow front and any edge trim. For the tied back panels, measure the back of the pillow. Cut two panels, each equal to the pillow height plus 1" (2.5 cm) and half of the pillow width plus 1¼" (3.3 cm). Cut two facing strips 2½" (6.3 cm) wide in the same length as the cut height of the panels. For a creative touch you can also place the opening off center on the pillow back, as shown.

2. Plan to place two or three evenly spaced sets of ties across the opening. Cut a 2" x 8" (5 cm x 20 cm) strip of fabric for each tie.

3. To make each tie, press under ¼" (6 mm) on one end of the fabric strip. Press the strip in half lengthwise to mark the center, then open it. Press the long edges under to meet in the center. Press the strip in half lengthwise, encasing the raw edges.

4. Edgestitch the open edges together.

5. The tied edges will overlap ¼" (6 mm). Press the edges that will be tied under in doubled ¼" (6 mm) hems, but do not stitch. Insert the raw tie end under the fold and pin or fuse in place with basting tape.

6. Press the tie over the hem and pin in place. Repeat for each tie, making sure the sets are aligned. Edgestitch the hems and ties in place.

7. Follow the instructions for the pillow sham style to assemble and finish the sham.

YOU WILL NEED

- decorator fabric
- cotton batting
- lining
- buttons or hook-and-loop tape (optional)
- disappearing fabric marker or chalk, if making flanged sham

DECORATIVE OPTIONS

Like pillows, pillow shams can be embellished with trims or pieced for an interesting look.

How to Make a Decorative Sham

Create a pieced or patchwork panel in the same manner as a pieced duvet cover.

1. Draw the cut size of the front panel on paper. Use a clear ruler and pencil to draw the patchwork design of your choice on the paper. Cut the pieces from assorted fabrics, adding ¼" (6 mm) seam allowances all around. Sew the pieces together, referring to your diagram. Complete the sham following the basic sham instructions on page 156.

2. To make a pillowcase-style sham with trim, measure the pillow. Cut two panels, making each 1" (2.5 cm) more than the pillow height and 4½" (11.3 cm) more than the pillow width. Sew the panels together along one long edge and one short edge. Press the open edges under in a doubled ½" (1.3 cm) hem and topstitch in place. Sew fringe along the edge, then sew the remaining long edges together. If desired, sew strips of flat trim across the sham before stitching the final seam.

Preprint Panel

A preprint panel makes a perfect center panel for a pillow sham when you add borders. Depending on the size of the panel, it can be used for standard size pillows or large square Euro shams. The panel shown is ideal for a Euro sham.

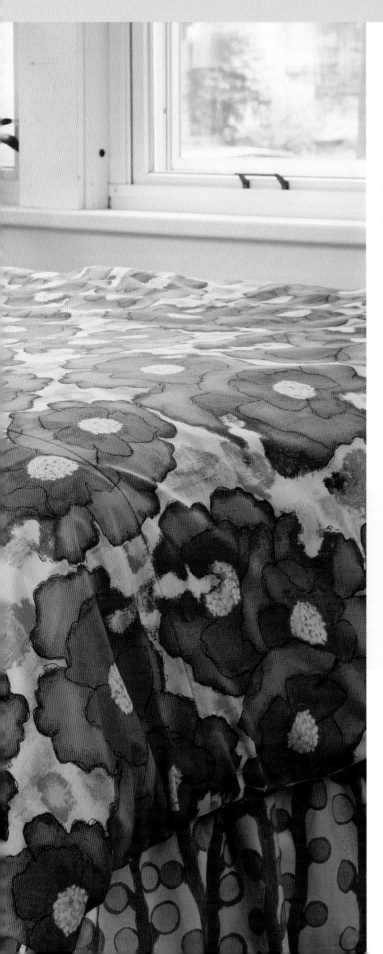

Bed Skirts

A bed skirt covers the box spring and legs of the bed frame and should complement the duvet cover or coverlet. The skirt can be tailored with pleats or gathered for a more casual look. Customize the design by placing pleats or gathers only at the corners or at the center of each side as well. For a bed with a footboard or posts, make the skirt with openings at the foot corners. In the instructions that follow, the bed skirt is attached to a fitted sheet, which covers the box spring. This method ensures that the skirt will stay in place when you make the bed or change sheets.

YOU WILL NEED

- fitted sheet in same size as bed
- decorator fabric
- water-soluble fabric marker

WHAT YOU NEED TO KNOW

A bed skirt is usually added to a platform—a piece of muslin or a fitted sheet that covers the box spring and lies under the mattress. It should be the exact size of the box spring so it will not show.

You can also attach a bed skirt by hemming the top edge in a ½" (1.3 cm) hem and sewing the loop side of hook-and-loop tape to the hemmed edges. Hand sew the loop side of the tape along the top edge of the box spring then attach the tapes.

Bed skirt lengths are not standard, so be sure to measure. To determine the finished size of the platform, measure the width and length of the box spring. To determine the finished height of the bed skirt side and end panels, measure from the top of the box spring to the floor. Measure the length of each side from the head of the bed to the foot for the finished side width of each side panel. Measure the foot of the bed from side to side to determine the finished end panel width.

If you must piece the sides or ends, be sure to match prints to make the seams less noticeable. If possible, plan to hide seams in pleats. If you are using a solid-color fabric or one without a directional print, you may be able to railroad the fabric. This means the panels are cut on the lengthwise grain, so you can eliminate unsightly seams along the sides.

How to Make a Tailored Bed Skirt with Center and Corner Pleats

This tailored style features deep 6" (15 cm) box pleats at each corner and 3" (7.5 cm) box pleats at the center of each side. For a full-size or larger bed, you may also want to add a center pleat to the end panel of the skirt.

1. Remove the mattress from the bed. Measure the box spring and add 1" (2.5 cm) to each dimension for seam allowances. Cut a rectangle of muslin or sheeting for the platform or use a fitted sheet. Place the platform fabric on the box spring or wrap the sheet over the box spring. Use a water-soluble fabric marker to mark the center of each side, the end (except for twin size), and the corners of the box spring. Mark the edges of the box spring on the sheet.

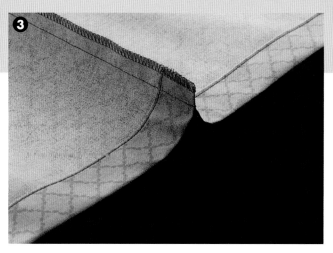

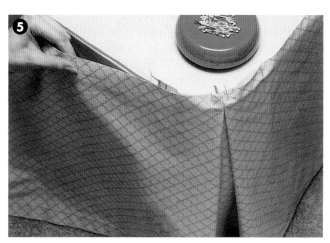

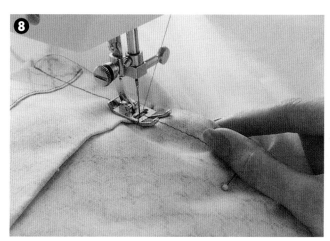

2. Determine the finished measurements for the skirt panels. Add 2" (5 cm) to the finished height for the cut height of the skirt. To determine the cut width of the panels, add together the finished widths for the side and end panels. Add 12" (30.5 cm) pleat allowance for each corner pleat and 6" (15 cm) pleat allowance for each center pleat. Also add 1" (2.5 cm) for each seam that will need to sewn to achieve the finished width. Also add 2" (5 cm) for the skirt side hems. *Note:* If possible, piece the panels together so the seams will be hidden in the pleats.

3. Cut the fabric pieces in the sizes determined and sew the short ends of the panels together. Sew together the seam allowances with serging or zigzag stitches. Press to one side.

4. Press the short ends under in a doubled ½" (1.3 cm) hem and topstitch. Press the bottom edge of the skirt under in a doubled 1" (2.5 cm) hem and topstitch in place.

5. Position the bed skirt so the center of the fabric aligns with the center of the foot of the box spring. For all sizes except a twin bed, make a box pleat at the center of the foot with

pleats 1½" (3.8 cm) deep on each side; pin in place. Pin the seam allowance on the top edge of the skirt into the box spring from the center, working toward the corners. At each corner, fold a box pleat with a pleat 3" (7.5 cm) deep on each side. Continue pinning the skirt seam allowance to the top of the box spring, folding and pinning the center pleats in place.

6. Remove the bed skirt from the box spring, repositioning the pins to secure the pleats. Press the pleats in place, with even pleat depth from the upper edge to the lower edge. Machine-baste ½" (1.3 cm) from the upper edge to secure the pleats.

7. Lay the skirt right-side down on top of the box spring. Pin the upper edge of the bed skirt to the sheet, extending ½" (1.3 cm) beyond the marked line.

8. Remove the bed skirt and fitted sheet from the box spring. Stitch the bed skirt to the sheet, using a ½" (1.3 cm) seam allowance. Finish the seam allowance with serging or zigzag stitches.

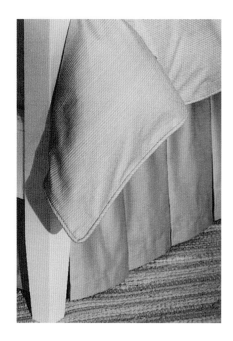

How to Make a Bed Skirt with Continuous Pleats

This tailored style features evenly spaced box pleats around the sides and foot of the bed.

1. Place a fitted sheet over the box spring. Using a water-soluble marker, mark the sheet along the upper edge of the box spring at each side and at the foot of the bed. Mark the corners at the center of the curve. Divide and mark the line along the edge of the box spring for evenly spaced pleats, 6" (15 cm) apart.

2. Determine the finished measurements for the side and end skirt panels. Add 2" (5 cm) to the finished height for the cut height of the panels. To determine the cut width of each panel, multiply the width of the box spring side or end by three and add 12" (30.5 cm). Cut the three panels from fabric.

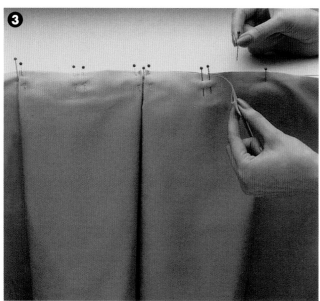

3. Press and stitch a 1" (2.5 cm) doubled hem in the bottom edge of each skirt panel. Pin the center of the skirt end panel top seam allowance to the box spring at the center of the foot end. Fold pleats in place at each mark, working from the center of the foot to the corners. The depth on each side of the pleat should equal the distance between the pleats. Pin to the box spring with the seam allowance extending above the upper edge.

4. At the corners, trim the fabric 3½" (8.75 cm) beyond the pleat fold line so the seam will be concealed in the pleat. Pin the side piece to the foot piece, pinning along the ½" (1.3 cm) seam allowance. Pin pleats in place on the side of the bed. Repeat for the other side.

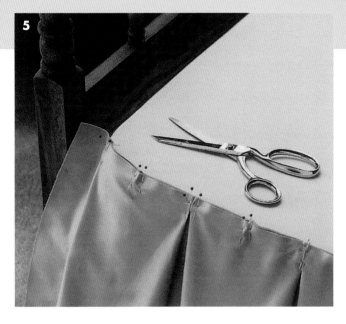

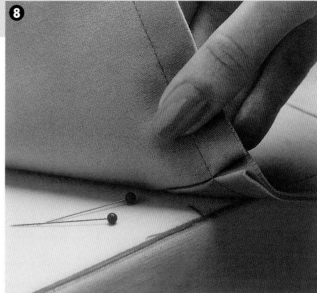

5. Trim the fabric 2" (5 cm) beyond the desired end point at the head of the bed. Pin doubled 1" (2.5 cm) hems in place.

6. Remove the skirt from the box spring, repositioning the pins to secure the pleats. Press the pleats in place, with even pleat depth from the upper edge to the lower edge.

7. Machine-baste the pleats in place ½" (1.25 cm) from the upper edges.

8. Lay the bed skirt right-side down on top of the box spring. Pin the upper edge of the bed skirt to the fitted sheet, extending the ½" (1.3 cm) seam allowance beyond the marked line.

9. Remove the bed skirt and fitted sheet from the bed. Stitch the bed skirt to the sheet, working ½" (1.3 cm) from the raw edge; finish the seam allowance with serging or zigzag stitches.

How to Make a Pleated Bed Skirt with Foot Corner Openings

1. Follow steps 1 through 3 for the continuous pleated skirt. At each end of the foot panel, trim the fabric 2" (5 cm) beyond the pleat fold line to allow for a doubled 1" (2.5 cm) side hem. Press the hem under and pin in place.

2. Pin the side hem in place on the next bed skirt piece. Align the hemmed edges together at the corner; pin. Pin the pleats in place on the side of the bed. Repeat for the other side.

3. Finish the bed skirt by following steps 5 through 9 for the continuous pleated skirt instructions above.

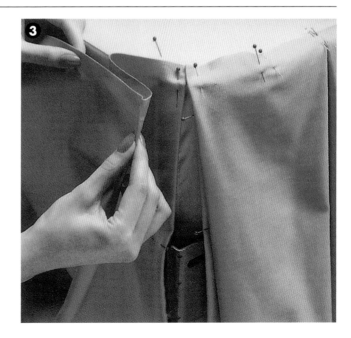

How to Make a Bed Skirt with Continuous Gathers

1. Place a fitted sheet over the box spring. Using a water-soluble fabric marker, mark the sheet along the edges of the box spring on each edge and at the foot of the bed. This will be the stitching line for the bed skirt. Mark another line ½" (1.3 cm) on the outside of the first line for a placement line.

2. Referring to the measuring instructions (page 164), add 2½" (6.3 cm) to the finished height measurement for the cut height of the skirt panels. Measure the total length of the marked line on the sheet and multiply by 2 to 2.5 (depending on fullness desired) to find the total cut finished width of the skirt panels. For example, the total inches for two sides and the end of the featured twin-size dust ruffle was 192" x 2 = 384" (487.7 cm x 2 = 975.4 cm); 384" divided by 42" (fabric width) = 9.14 (975.4 cm divided by 106.7 cm = 9.14) widths needed. Round up to 10 to allow for seam allowances and side hems. For this dust ruffle 14" (35.5 cm) long, 10 fabric panels, each 16½" x 42" (41.9 x 106.7 cm) were cut and pieced together. Cut fabric panels in the determined height to achieve the total width.

3. Sew the short edges of the skirt panels together. Press the seam allowances open. Press the bottom and side edges of the skirt under in a doubled 1" (2.5 cm) hem and top-stitch in place.

4. Divide the upper edge of the skirt and the marked line on the fitted sheet on the box spring into fourths and mark with pins.

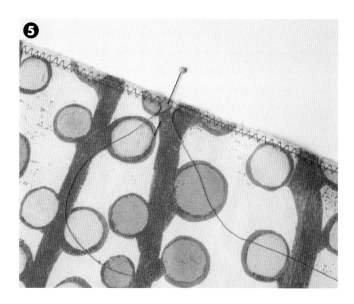

5. Using a separate length of cord for each marked section of the skirt top, zigzag stitch over heavyweight thread or lightweight cord on the right side of the skirt panels, ⅜" (1 cm) from the upper edge.

6. Place the skirt right-side down on top of the box spring, matching the marks; pin the upper edge of the skirt to the sheet at the quarter marks, aligning the gathered skirt edge with the outside line. Secure one end of each gathering thread by wrapping it securely around a pin. Pull the remaining end of the thread to evenly gather the skirt between the pins; pin the gathers in place.

7. Carefully remove the pinned bed skirt and fitted sheet from the box spring. Sew the bed skirt to the sheet, stitching ½" (1.3 cm) from the raw skirt edge. Finish the seam allowance with serging or zigzag stitches if desired.

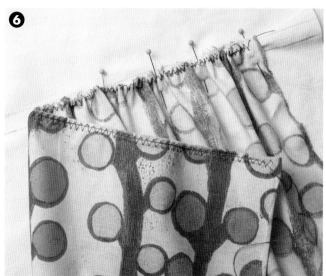

How to Make a Gathered Bed Skirt with Corner Openings

1. Follow steps 1 through 4 on page 168 to cut and assemble the skirt, except stitch the side and end panels in three sections.

2. Mark the corners on the fitted sheet placed over the box spring. Divide the upper edge of each skirt section in half and mark. Divide the marked line on the fitted sheet in half on each side and at the foot of the bed and mark.

3. Lay the skirt right-side down on the box spring, matching the marks and extending the skirt seam allowance over the marked line. Pin the skirt to the box spring at the marks, being careful not to catch the cords.

4. Pull the cords to evenly gather the skirt between the marks. Pin the skirt to the sheet, extending the seam allowance on the skirt past the marked line.

5. Remove the sheet from the box spring. Sew the bed skirt to the sheet, stitching ½" (1.3 cm) from the raw edge. Finish the seam allowance with serging or zigzag stitches.

Bedspreads and Coverlets

Like a duvet cover, your bedspread or coverlet is one of the main components of a beautiful bedroom. While duvet covers are made to encase a comforter, bedspreads and coverlets are used alone as a bed covering. Bedspreads are floor length, while coverlets are shorter and are usually combined with a bed skirt.

WHAT YOU NEED TO KNOW

Bedspreads and coverlets can be the easiest bed coverings to make. They are thinner than a decorative comforter or a comforter encased by a duvet cover and can be made with a single layer of fabric or lined. You can also add low-loft batting to lined versions of either style and embellish with quilting, if desired.

A bedspread completely covers the bed and tucks under the pillows with sides that extend to just above the floor. It can be lined or unlined and is usually made with medium- to heavyweight fabrics. Fabrics that look nice on both sides, such as fleece, matelassé, double-sided quilted fabrics, and yarn-dyed woven fabrics work best for unlined bedspreads. Choose lighter weight fabric if you will be making a fitted bedspread with a gathered skirt.

YOU WILL NEED

- decorator fabric
- plate or other round object, if making rounded corners
- chalk or water-soluble fabric marker
- lining (optional)
- batting (optional)
- fringe (optional)
- fusible fleece

How to Determine Fabric Requirements and Cut Pieces

Refer to the Bedding Size Chart on page 143 to measure the bed for a throw-style bedspread or coverlet.

1. To determine the cut length of the fabric, measure the mattress length from the head to the foot. Add the desired drop length at the foot (1"–4" [2.5–10 cm] below the mattress for a duvet or coverlet or to ½" [1.3 cm] above the floor for a bedspread). For lined covers, add 1" (2.5 cm) for seam allowance; for unlined covers, add 4" (10 cm) for doubled 1" (2.5 cm) hems. For a bedspread, also add an 18" (45.7 cm) pillow tuck allowance.

2. To determine the cut width of the fabric (after piecing), measure the mattress width from side to side. Add double the drop length. For lined covers, add 1" (2.5 cm) for seam allowances; for unlined covers, add 4" (10 cm) for doubled 1" (2.5 cm) hems. Divide the cut width by the width of the fabric and round up to the nearest whole number to determine the number of fabric widths needed.

3. Multiply the cut length by the number of panels needed. Divide by 36 (100) to determine the number of yards (meters) required for the bedspread or coverlet. Allow extra fabric (full print repeat) if you will be matching a print at the seam lines. This is for the top layer only; for a reversible cover or lined cover you will need the same amount of fabric for the bottom layer.

How to Measure the Bed for a Fitted Bedspread

1. Measure the length of the mattress top and add 18" (45.7 cm) for a pillow tuck allowance. Add 2½" (6.3 cm) for seam allowances; this is the cut length of the top panel. Measure the width of the mattress top and add 1" (2.5 cm) for seam allowances; this is the cut width of the top panel. If the fabric will be pieced, add 1" (2.5 cm) to the width for each seam.

2. For fitted side and end panels with corner pleats, measure from the top of the bed to the floor and add 1½" (3.8 cm) for a hem allowance; this is the cut height of the panel. Measure the side of the mattress from the head to the foot. Add 2" (5 cm) for the top edge hem and 4½" (11.3 cm) for the end pleat. This is the cut width of each side panel. If you are using a directional print, the side panels will have to be pieced. For the end panel, measure the end of the mattress from side to side. Add 9" (23 cm) for a pleat allowance. The cut length is the same as the length of each side panel.

3. For gathered side and end panels, determine the cut height as for the fitted panels in step 2. For the cut width (including piecing) of the sides and ends, double the corresponding mattress measurements.

How to Make an Unlined Bedspread or Coverlet

1. Determine the measurements and cut sizes. For an unlined cover, cut two panels in the planned length. If you will be matching the print, cut one panel a full print repeat longer; this will be the panel to cut in half lengthwise.

2. Cut one panel in half lengthwise. Sew a half panel to each side of the full panel, matching the print if applicable (see matching prints for duvet covers on page 145). Finish the seams with serging or zigzag stitches.

3. Finish the upper edges of the bedspread with serging or zigzag stitches, then press under 2" (5 cm). Topstitch the hem in place close to the inner edge of the hem.

(continued)

4. To round the bottom corners, place a plate or another round object on the wrong side of one corner. Use chalk or a fabric marker to draw around the plate. Cut along the marked line. Use the trimmed corner as a pattern to cut the remaining corner.

5. To hem the side and bottom edges of the bedspread or coverlet, finish the edges with serging or zigzag stitches. Press under a doubled 1" (2.5 cm) hem and topstitch in place.

6. To bind the side and bottom edges instead of hemming, eliminate the hem allowance when cutting the fabric pieces. Refer to page 186 to cut bias strips 2¼" (5.8 cm) wide and equal in length to the total length of the edges to be bound plus 6" (15 cm). Sew the bias strips together using a ¼" (6 mm) seam allowance. Press the seams open. Press one end under ½" (1.3 cm), then press the strip in half lengthwise with wrong sides together. Pin the folded strip to the right side of the cover, aligning the raw edges and the finished end of the bias strip at one end of the edge to be bound. Sew in place ¼" (6 mm) from the edge.

7. Wrap the fold to the lining side and slipstitch in place.

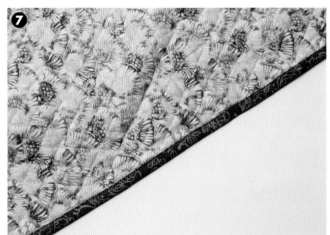

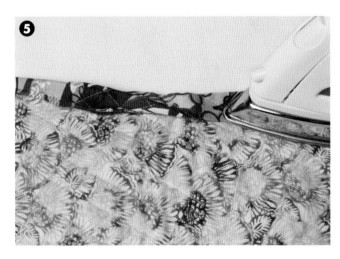

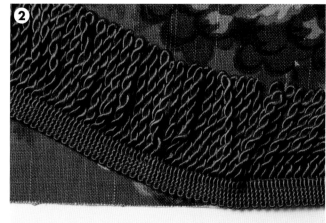

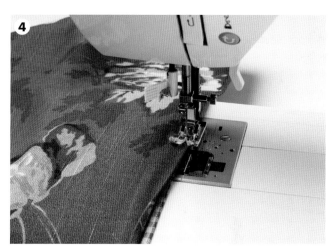

How to Make a Lined Bedspread or Coverlet with Fringe

1. Follow steps 1 and 2 for the unlined bedspread or coverlet to cut and piece the top panel, matching prints as necessary (page 182). Repeat for the lining fabric. If desired, cut a piece of low-loft batting the same size. *Note:* Subtract the 2" (5 cm) top hem allowance from the cut length of the panels. Also adjust the cut width and length if you are adding fringe to a bedspread.

2. With the raw edges even, baste the fringe header to the right side of the bedspread top, stitching along the inside edge of the fringe header.

3. Place the pieced lining right-side up on a flat surface and lay the pieced top right-side down on the lining with edges and seams aligned. If you are adding batting, layer it on the wrong side of the pieced top. Pin, then sew the layers together, stitching along the fringe stitching line on the side and bottom edges. Leave an opening for turning in the top edge.

4. Turn the bedspread or coverlet right-side out and press. Press under the seam allowances on the opening. Topstitch close to the top edge, stitching the opening closed.

5. For a bedspread or coverlet with batting, stitch the layers together by stitching around motifs or in a grid across the width and length if desired.

How to Make a Fitted Bedspread with Pleated Corners

The top panel of a fitted bedspread can be left unlined, or it can be lined with or without the addition of batting.

1. Determine the measurements and cut sizes of the panels as instructed on page 172. Cut the top panel pieces from fabric, adding 16" (45.5 cm) to the total width of the skirt for an 8" (20 cm) pleat allowance at each corner of the foot of the bed. Also cut the top panel pieces from lining fabric and fusible fleece or lightweight batting. Fuse or baste the fleece or batting to the wrong side of the top panel.

2. Piece the top panel, matching a large print at the seam lines, if used. Repeat for the lining fabric. If desired, apply trim along the seam.

3. Piece the skirt panels for each side and the end to achieve the necessary width.

4. With raw edges even and the skirt ends aligned with the top of the bedspread's top panel, pin the side panels to the top panel 4" (10 cm) from each bottom corner. To make each corner pleat, fold and press pleats 2" (5 cm) deep to meet at the corner. Continue pinning the skirt to the bottom edge of the bedspread top. If necessary, adjust the pleat depth for a smooth fit. Make sure the center of each pleat is aligned with the corner. Clip the seam allowance at the center of the pleat to smoothly turn the corner

5. Sew the skirt to the top, pressing the pleat to the bottom of the skirt.

6. Turn right-side out and press.

7. Finish all edges with serging or zigzag stitches. Press the top edge of the skirt and top panel under 2" (5 cm) and topstitch in place.

8. Place the bedspread on the bed and mark the hemline ½" to 1" (1.3 to 2.5 cm) above the floor. Press under a doubled hem and topstitch in place. Sew trim to the edge if desired.

How to Make a Fitted Bedspread with Gathered Skirt

1. Follow steps 1 through 3 for the fitted bedspread with corner pleats to cut and assemble the top and side panels (page 176).

2. Sew the short ends of the skirt panels together to achieve the total determined width.

3. To gather the skirt, zigzag stitch over cording ⅜" (1 cm) from the edge. Pin-mark the perimeter of the top panel side and bottom edges in fourths. Repeat for the top edge of the skirt.

4. With raw edges aligned and the ends of the skirt even with the top edge of the top panel, pin the skirt to the top at the ends and at the pin marks. Be careful not to catch the gathering threads in the pins.

5. Pull the gathering threads to gather the skirt to fit the top panel. Pin the gathers in place. Sew the skirt to the top.

6. Follow steps 6 through 8, opposite, to finish the bedspread.

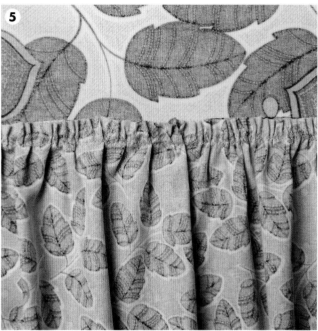

How to Add Batting and Line the Top Panel of a Bedspread

1. Cut a rectangle of batting and a rectangle of lining fabric, each in the cut dimensions of the bedspread top panel.

2. After the skirt is sewn to the top panel, but before the upper edge is hemmed, place the bedspread on a large, flat surface with the top right-side up and the skirt wrong-side up and toward the center of the top panel.

3. Layer the lining panel right-side down on the bedspread with the top panel and lining edges even and the skirt sandwiched between the layers. Place the batting on top of the lining. Pin the layers together around the side and bottom edges.

4. Sew the layers together. Turn right-side out and press. Finish the upper edge of the batting and lining with the top panel, treating them as one and following the bedspread with skirt instructions.

TECHNICAL SUPPORT

Choosing the Right Fabrics

When selecting fabrics for your slipcovers, pillows, and bedding, consider what effect you want these décor pieces to have in the room. While color and design play an important part in the decision, it is also important to consider the fiber content, weave structure, and any surface treatment applied to the fabric.

You should make your slipcovers with decorator fabrics. These differ from fashion fabrics in several ways. Decorator fabrics are generally more durable than fashion fabrics. Often they are treated with a stain-resistant or crease-resistant finish. For this reason, most decorator fabrics must be dry cleaned rather than laundered—a point that is especially important for slipcovers because shrinkage can be disastrous. Unlike fashion fabrics, decorator fabrics with designs are printed or woven to match from one selvage to the next, so that any necessary seams in large pieces are less visible. The fabric identification label gives the measurement of the pattern repeats. The vertical repeat is the distance up and down between points where the pattern repeats itself. The horizontal repeat is often given also, especially for larger prints. This information is necessary for determining the amount of fabric needed for a slipcover. Large motifs in a pattern must be centered on cushion tops and bottoms, chair backs, and arms. Ideally, a pattern should flow uninterrupted from the top to the bottom of the slipcover. Likewise, large motifs should be centered on pillows and pillow shams, and the print should be matched across seams in bedspreads, coverlets, and duvet covers.

The scale of a print is also an important consideration. Large prints may overpower a small chair slipcover or a bean bag chair, just as tiny all-over prints can get lost on a large sofa slipcover or bedspread. If you want to use several prints in the same room, select coordinating prints in various sizes, and add solid color accents.

Fabrics can be grouped into categories according to their weave or surface design. Plain weaves (1) are the simplest of weaves. They may be solid in color or printed, and their strength is determined by the closeness of the yarns in the weave. Satin weaves (2) are woven so that yarns float on the surface, giving the fabric a subtle sheen. They also may be solid in color or printed. Jacquard weaves (3), including damasks, tapestries, and brocades, have woven-in designs. Novelty weaves (4), often single colors, feature textural interest created by complicated weave patterns. These fabrics are very versatile in any color scheme. Pile fabrics (5), such as suede, corduroy, and chenille, have interesting surface textures.

Decorator fabrics for the interior are often made of natural fibers, which include cotton, linen, silk, and wool. Natural fibers are breathable, comfortable, and easy to sew. Unfortunately, these fabrics don't perform very well for porches, sunrooms, or outdoors. To keep up with the strong trend toward outdoor decorating, manufacturers are also making water-repellent, fade-resistant, acrylic or polyester decorator fabrics that look and feel like interior fabrics. They are colorfast and are treated to resist stains and mildew. Performance fabrics intended for outdoor use look and feel like interior decorator fabrics and are available in some of the same prints and colors.

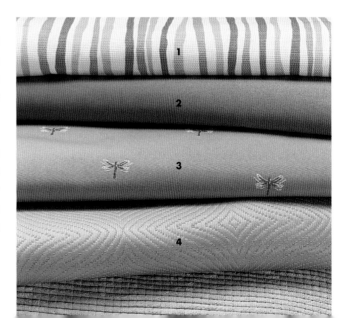

FABRIC REQUIREMENTS FOR SLIPCOVERING FURNITURE

ITEM	AMOUNT OF FABRIC NEEDED
Chairs	
0 Cushion	7 yd (6.4 m)
1 Cushion	8 yd (7.3 m)
2 Cushion	10 yd (9.1 m)
Wing Chair	
1 Cushion	9 yd (8.2 m)
Boudoir Chair	5 yd (4.6 m)
Wing Chair	
0 Cushion	5½ yd (5 m)
1 Cushion	7½ yd (6.9 cm)
Dining Room Chairs	
Seats	1 yd (1 m)
Backs	1 yd (1 m)
Ottoman	
0 Cushion	2½ yd (2.3 m)
1 Cushion	3½ yd (3.2 m)
Folding Chairs	3½ yd (3.2 m)
Sofa	
2 or 3 Seat Cushion Only (No Back Cushion)	18 yd (16.5 m)
2 Seat and 2 Back	20 yd (18.3 m)
3 Seat and 3 Back	22 yd (20.1 m)
4 Seat and 4 Back	25 yd (23 m)
3 Seat and 3 Back (2 Bolsters)	23 yd (21 m)
4 Seat and 4 Back (2 Bolsters)	25 yd (23 m)
Love Seat	
Up to 60" (1.5 m), 2 Seat Cushions	14 yd (12.8 m)
2 Seat and 2 Back	16 yd (14.6 m)

ITEM	AMOUNT OF FABRIC NEEDED
Chaise Lounge	
0 Cushion	14 yd (12.8 m)
1 Cushion	14 yd (12.8 m)
2 Cushion	14 yd (12.8 m)
Studio Couch	
1 Piece	8½ yd (7.8 m)
Cap Only	4½ yd (4.1 m)
Duster Only	7½ yd (6.9 m)
Bolster	1½ yd (1.4 m)
Mattress Cover	5 yd (4.6 m)
Sectional Sofa – Sofa Size	
No Arm, 1 Cushion	13 yd (11.9 m)
1 Arm, 1 Cushion	14½ yd (13.3 m)
Love Seat Size	
No Arm, 1 Cushion	9 yd (8.2 m)
1 Arm, 1 Cushion	11½ yd (10.5 m)
Chair Size	
No Arm, 1 Cushion	7 yd (6.4 m)
1 Arm, 1 Cushion	8 yd (7.3 m)
Headboards	
Twin	4 yd (3.7 m)
Double	5 yd (4.6 m)
Queen	6 yd (5.5 m)
King	6 yd (5.5 m)

These fabric requirements are based on standard size furniture, 54" (137 cm) fabric with up to 27" (68.6 cm) pattern repeat.

Construction Basics

Whether you are making simple dining chair covers or a more complicated fitted slipcover for a sofa, there are some basic techniques you'll use over and over. Follow these guidelines for successful results.

LAYING OUT AND CUTTING THE FABRIC

Whenever possible, lay out all the pattern pieces on the fabric before you start to cut. This allows you to rearrange the pieces as necessary to make the best use of the fabric.

When a patterned fabric with an all-over design is used for slipcovers, little matching is required. When seaming widths of fabric together, such as for a sofa, the pattern should be matched. Patterned fabrics can also be matched at the seam line on the upper edge of the skirt,

if desired, following the technique for boxed cushions (page 122). If a patterned fabric with a one-way design is used, take care to lay the pieces in the correct direction of the fabric.

Center large motifs in a print fabric on the top and bottom of the cushion. For best results, also align the design so it continues down the back of the furniture, onto the cushion, and down the skirt.

Laying Out and Cutting the Slipcover Fabric

• Center large motifs, such as floral clusters, on the back, sides, and cushions, and on the top of the arms.

• Center the prominent stripe of a striped fabric on the center placement line of the outside and inside back pieces and on the cushion pieces. Decide which direction the stripes will run on the arms; usually it looks best to have the stripes run in the same direction as the stripes on the skirt.

• Cut the skirt pieces for a self-lined skirt, placing the fold line at the lower edge of the skirt on a crosswise fold of the fabric. Self-lined skirts hang better than single-layer skirts with a hem.

• Cut arm pieces, right sides together, using the first piece as the pattern for cutting the second piece.

• Mark names of pieces on the wrong side of the fabric, using chalk. Abbreviations like "D" for deck, "IB" for inside back, and "OA" for outside arm work well.

• Transfer all markings, including notches and dots, from the muslin pieces to the slipcover fabric.

HOW TO MATCH A PATTERNED FABRIC

1. Position fabric widths, right sides together, matching selvages. Fold back the upper selvage until the pattern matches; lightly press fold line.

2. Unfold the selvage; pin fabric widths together on the fold line. Check match from the right side.

3. Re-pin the fabric widths so pins are perpendicular to the fold line; stitch on the fold line, using a straight stitch. Trim fabric to finished length.

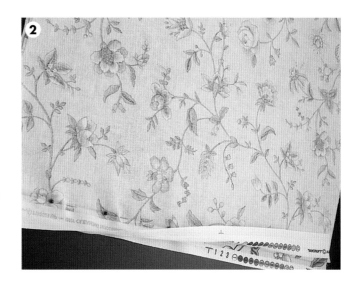

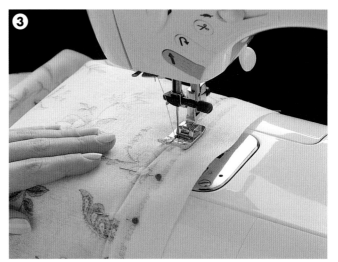

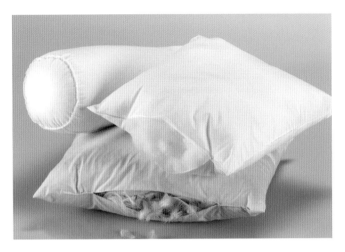

Forms and Fillings

Pillows get their shape from natural or synthetic fillings. Depending on the shape, size, and purpose of a pillow, you can fill it with loose filling or with a pillow form. Forms are great for pillows that will be laundered or dry cleaned because they are easily inserted and removed through a zippered or lapped closure. If you want to be able to remove the filling for cleaning a pillow that is a nonstandard size or shape, make a muslin-covered form in the same shape as the pillow and fill it with the desired material. Loose filling can be stuffed directly into the pillow cover if you intend to stitch it closed.

Forms are available in knife-edge squares from 10" to 30" (25.5 to 76 cm), rectangles, rounds, and bolsters. The most expensive forms are filled with down or a mix of down and feathers. Down-filled pillows can be shaped and slouched to conform to the corner of a sofa. They mold comfortably to your body when you lean on them, but they are brought back to billowy plumpness with a little fluffing. Polyester fiberfill forms imitate some features of down, but they are more resilient or springy than down. Fiberfill forms are lower in cost, washable, and nonallergenic. Different brands of fiberfill forms vary in quality and price—some are more plump, guaranteed not to separate or clump, and have fabric covers as opposed to thin nonwoven synthetic covers.

Manufactured forms aren't necessarily ready for use, especially if they seem high through the center with filling that doesn't reach the corners. You can open a seam and adjust the filling, if necessary, filling out the corners and creating a more even thickness. If you want more plumpness, add some loose fiberfill before sewing the form closed. To use a knife-edge form for a box or mock box pillow, move filling out of the corners and follow steps 3 and 4 for the Mock Box Pillow, page 127, stitching from the outside of the form.

Styrofoam pellets for filling bean bag chairs are packaged in large bags and sold at large fabric stores, some home goods and department stores, and online.

Making and Attaching Self Welt

Just as piping is used in garments to outline a fashion detail, welting is used in home décor sewing to define and support seams. Welting is fabric-covered cording, sewn into a seam to provide extra strength and a decorative finishing touch.

Fabric strips for welting can be cut on the bias or the straight grain. Straight-grain welting requires less fabric but is only suitable for seams that are straight because it is less flexible. Use bias fabric strips for welting that will be sewn around curves. Bias welting strips do not have to be cut on the true bias. Cutting the strips at an angle less than 45 degrees gives the flexibility of bias grain, but requires less fabric. For stripes and plaids, bias welting does not require matching. If you need to make several yards (meters) of welting, save time cutting and joining the strips by using the method on page 186.

Cording with a diameter of ⁵⁄₃₂" (3.8 mm) is the usual cording for cushions and slipcover seams. Cut the fabric strips 1½" (3.8 cm) wide. Cording with a diameter of ¼" (6 mm) is slightly larger for similar applications. Cut the fabric strips 1¾" (4.5 cm) wide. To determine how wide to cut the fabric strips on other sizes of cording, wrap a piece of fabric or paper around the cording. Pin it together, encasing the cording. Cut ½" (1.3 cm) from the pin. Measure the width, and cut strips to match.

The instructions below show you how to attach welting in a continuous circle, such as for a boxed cushion. When a welted seam will be intersected by another seam, remove ½" (1.3 cm) of the cording from the end of the welting to prevent bulk at the seam line.

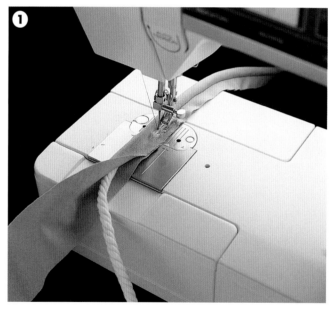

MAKING AND ATTACHING WELTING

1. Center the cording on the wrong side of the strip. Fold the strip over the cording, aligning the raw edges. Using a zipper foot, machine-baste close to the cording.

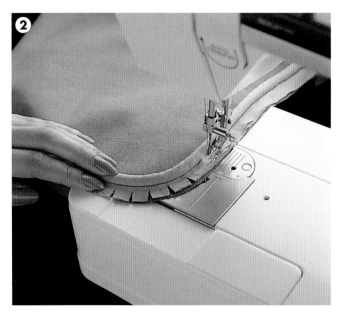

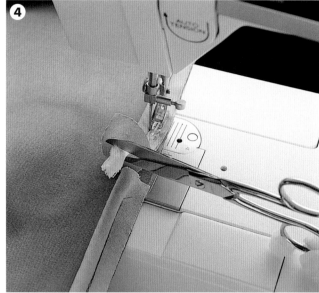

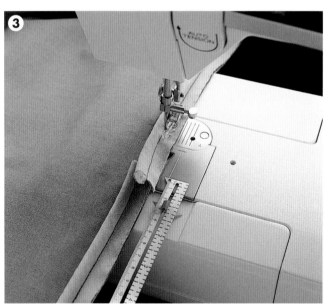

2. Attach the welting to the right side of the slipcover piece with raw edges aligned. Begin stitching 2" (5 cm) from the end of the welting; stitch on the basting line. To ease at rounded corners, clip into the seam allowances up to the basting. To prevent welted seams from puckering, take care not to stretch either welting or fabric as the seam is stitched.

3. Stop stitching 2" (5 cm) from the point where the cording ends will meet. Leaving the needle in the fabric, cut off one end so it overlaps the other end by 1" (2.5 cm).

4. Remove 1" (2.5 cm) of stitching from each end of the welting. Trim the cording ends so they just meet.

5. Fold under ½" (1.3 cm) of the overlapping fabric. Lap it around the other end; finish stitching.

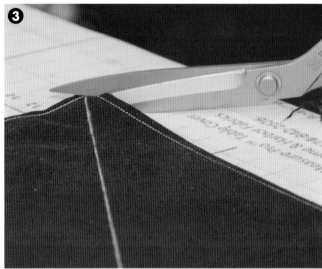

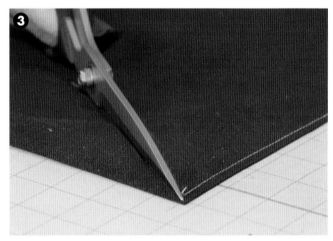

1. Cut a full width of 54" (137 cm) fabric 18" (45.7 cm) long. Fold the fabric in half with the wrong sides out. Sew ½" (1.3 cm) seams on the three open edges.

2. Trim seam allowances to ¼" (6 mm). Draw a line diagonally from corner to corner.

3. Snip off one corner, then cut on the marked line, from corner to corner, making sure to cut ONLY the top layer of fabric. Snip the end corner to finish the cut.

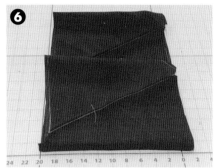

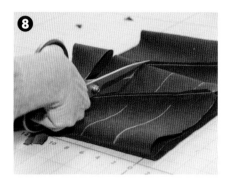

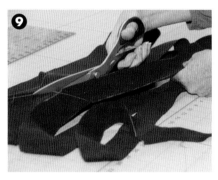

4. Flip fabric over and do the same thing on the opposite side, connecting the two UNSNIPPED corners, and again, cut ONLY the top layer of fabric. Snip these two corners, as in step 3.

5. Pull open the fabric where it has been cut. You should have a tube.

Use Scraps

With this method, one can make continuous bias out of rectangular scraps by sewing four sides of the fabric. Or, this can be done with smaller pieces of fabric for only one or two yards (meters) of bias.

6. Lay the fabric tube flat on the work surface, aligning cut edges. From the bottom, fold up two-thirds of the distance (this reduces cutting time) so the lower fold is about 6" (15 cm) from the top fold.

7. Draw lines from bottom to the first fold, making the lines 1½" (3.8 cm) apart (to cover ⁵⁄₃₂" [3.8 mm] cording with a ½" [1.3 cm] seam allowance).

8. Cut on these lines through all layers to make strips. Stop cutting once you've cut through the first fold.

9. Open the fabric. There will be a section that has not been cut. Lay this as flat as possible on the table. Beginning on the left edge, using a straightedge, draw a line *diagonally* from the outer edge of the fabric even with the end of the lower cuts to the end of the first upper cut. Continue connecting the ends of the cut lines at a slight diagonal. When you reach the right side, you will be connecting the final lower cut to the upper right edge. *Do not* draw straight lines connecting the cuts or you will end up with many circles instead of continuous bias. After all lines are marked diagonally, cut on the marked lines through the single layer only.

10. Presto! Like magic, there should be nearly 18 yds (16.5 m) of continuous bias strip to sew around ⁵⁄₃₂" (3.8 mm) cording.

Terms to Know

Bias: Any diagonal line intersecting the lengthwise and crosswise grains of fabric. While woven fabric is very stable on the lengthwise and crosswise grains, it has considerable stretch on the bias.

Crosswise grain: On woven fabrics, the crosswise grain is perpendicular to the selvages. Fabric has slight "give" in the crosswise grain.

Cut length: The total length at which fabric pieces should be cut for the slipcover. It includes allowances for any hems or seams.

Cut width: The total width at which the fabric should be cut. If more than one width of fabric is needed, the cut width refers to the entire panel after seams are sewn.

Darts: Intentional folds made and stitched in the fabric to remove excess fullness and give shape to an item. For instance, darts are sewn at the front corners of a chair seat cover to make the fabric conform to the front corners of the seat.

Directional print: The design printed on the fabric may have definite up and down directions, such as flowers growing upward. All pieces of a slipcover should be cut so that the print will run in the correct direction when you are finished.

Finish: To improve the durability of a seam, the raw edges are secured with stitches that prevent them from fraying. This can be done with zigzag stitches that wrap over the edge or with serging.

Lengthwise grain: On woven fabrics, the lengthwise grain runs parallel to the selvages. Fabrics are generally stronger along the lengthwise grain.

Lining: A fabric backing sewn to the underside of the face fabric to provide extra body.

Muslin: This medium-weight, plainly woven cotton fabric is relatively inexpensive, so it is often used for drafting patterns when paper isn't feasible.

Pattern repeat: The lengthwise distance from one distinctive point in the fabric pattern, such as the tip of a particular petal in a floral pattern, to the same point in the next pattern design.

Railroading: Normally the lengthwise grain of the fabric runs vertically in a slipcover. Since decorator fabric is usually 54" (137 cm) wide, slipcover pieces that are wider than this, such as skirts, must have vertical seams joining additional widths of fabric. Railroading means the fabric is turned sideways, so the lengthwise grain runs horizontally. The full width can then be cut in one piece, eliminating the need for any seams.

Self-lined: A fabric panel lined to the edge with the same fabric. Rather than cutting two pieces and sewing them together, one double-length piece is cut, folded with right sides together, and stitched on the remaining three sides so the lower edge will have a fold instead of a seam or hem.

Selvage: The narrow, tightly woven edges of the fabric that do not ravel or fray. These should be cut away on firmly woven fabrics before seaming to prevent puckering of seams.

ABOUT THE AUTHORS

Karen Erickson has been working in the home décor interior industry since 1986 when she started Fine Finishing by Karen, designing and fabricating draperies, slipcovers, and other fabric accessories. In 1998, her company became a corporation, and she changed its name to Slipcover America, Inc. Karen has worked with designers, decorators, and retail customers throughout the United States, specializing in on-site fabrication. Karen instructs both in the United States and Canada, doing seminars and workshops at fabric stores, for sewing guilds and groups, in professional workrooms, and at numerous trade shows. In January of 2007 she partnered with Claudia Buchanan of Sew What! to start www. HomeFashionsU.com.

Carol Zentgraf is a designer, writer, and editor specializing in sewing, fabrics, and decorating. She has a degree in art and interior design from Drake University and especially enjoys incorporating a variety of artistic techniques into her fabric projects. Carol has worked in the craft and sewing industries as both a designer and editor for more than thirty years and is the author of eight books. She is also a regular contributor to several magazines and websites. Carol lives in Illinois.

ACKNOWLEDGMENTS

The following people provided instruction and photography for slipcover projects in the book:

Teresa Bennett
(Office Task Chair)
Cozy Cottage Slipcovers
www.cozycottageslipcovers.com
(216) 749-1829

Therese M. Davis
(Barrel Chair, Open Arm Rocker)
Fabrications Studio
www.fabrications-studio.com
(847) 687-7064

The following companies provided products:

Coats & Clark
www.coatsandclark.com
thread and zippers

Dritz/Prym Consumer USA
www.dritz.com
Wonder Tape basting tape, tools

Expo International
www.atreasurenest.com
trims

Fabri Quilt
www.fabri-quilt.com
reversible quilted fabric

Fairfield Processing Corp.
www.poly-fil.com
batting and Soft Touch pillow forms

Free Spirit Fabrics
www.westminsterfibers.com
fabric

Michael Miller Fabrics
www.michaelmillerfabrics.com
fabric

Rowan Fabrics
www.westminsterfibers.com
fabric

Warm Company
www.warmcompany.com
Steam a Seam 2 fusible web sheets
and tape

Index

b

c

d